I FORGIVE MY FATHER

THE JOURNEY TO PERFECTING FORGIVENESS

JOHN W. WILSON II

JOHN W. WILSON II

CONTENTS

Published by John W. Wilson, II

Website: www.jwwilsonii.com

This novel is entirely a work of nonfiction. Other than the author himself, the names and characters portrayed are fictional for the protection of their identity, however, incidents portrayed in it are the product of the author's remembrance. Any resemblance to actual persons, living or dead, or events or localities is entirely coincidental.

DEDICATION

I dedicate this book to my 1st born son, Judah and my nephew, Da'Shawn. Judah, I'm honored God chose me to be the father of a world changing son. Da'Shawn, I am so, so proud of you. What should have broken you only revealed your strengths. May the Spirit and heart of the Father rest on you both all the days of your life. Words will never adequately explain how much I love you.

MY PRAYER

God I know I didn't write this book just to be titled an author or to have another accomplishment. You inspired this book for a particular people for this exact time. Now Father, I pray that every person that You desire to read this book does and their heart is open to what You have to say. I pray that every eye that reads this book and every ear that hears words from this book be opened to the power of forgiveness. I pray that every stronghold of unforgiveness, bitterness, anger, resentment, frustration, abandonment and rejection is broken by the blood of Jesus and power of the name of Jesus. Let it be broken over every person and every broken relationship, whether it's father and son/daughter, mother and son/daughter, husband and wife, family members, friends, coworkers or strangers. Please let this book change mindsets and perspectives on unforgiveness. May You reveal the power and authority we have over unforgiveness and teach us how to apply it to our daily lives. Heal our hearts and renew our minds so that we are free to pursue our purpose...We thank you in advance! Amen!

1

IN THE BEGINNING

My parents grew up in a small country area. The type of area where everybody knows your name, and if they don't, they know someone who does. Their households included both parents that knew each other most of their lives. They went to elementary school together but didn't get to know each other until high school. Although they were in the same grade, my mother was about six months older than my father. They grew up and lived almost contrary lives. My father was the only child, and my mother was the second oldest and only girl of four. They lived in, what was considered, a low-income country area with little wealth. The primary source of employment was "chicken plants" or poultry processing plants, which gives an idea of what the economic status was for that area. Neither my mother nor father's family had very much money but my father at the time was living in a two-room shack with his parents.

Randomly, one day in high school, my father's friend asked him, "Who would you marry"? I guess that's what high school students asked each other back then. My father made it known that he would marry my mother. According to my mother, he was a charming nice young man, well-dressed, and professional, even in high school. It wasn't odd for him to wear a shirt and tie to school. I guess the charm and fancy clothes, were part of the reason he won my mother over and they began dating.

At the beginning of their relationship, my father was ashamed to take my mother to his home. Not long after they began dating, my father's parents were able to move into a mobile home. Mobile homes were a popular choice back then in my community. I believe the move by my paternal grandparents was greatly influenced by my father and his shame in their living situation.

During the 11th grade, my parents began to seriously date. That sounds like the making of a beautiful love story...but the love story didn't turn out to be that beautiful. What started as a beautiful love story would soon become an on and off relationship because of my father's infidelity. The infidelity would continue throughout the relationship and later into the marriage. Despite their challenges, they attended the 11th grade prom together. However, they did not participate in their Senior Prom together. They continued their courtship on and off throughout high school as my mother aided my father in completing the 12th grade and graduating. Her efforts were not in vain, as they both graduated in 1972.

After graduation, my mother decided to attend Business School in Washington, D.C., and also continued a relationship with my father. While my mother was in college furthering her education, she would hear stories of my father taking other girls to the drive-in movies. Although that was a distraction, it didn't stop her from completing business school or maintaining a relationship with my father, despite transferring schools to be closer to home.

In September 1974, my father joined the Army and in the same month, my parents got married. After they were married, my father's service in Germany began. My mother joined him in October of 1974. My parents stayed in Germany for seventeen months and missed two Christmases at home. The time in Germany seemed to be a good and promising start to their marriage. In 1976, they returned to the States and moved in with my father's parents. Not long after they were back in the States, infidelity began to create issues in their relationship once again.

The infidelity eventually led my mother to move back in with her parents. During the time my mother was living with her parents, she found out she was pregnant with... you guessed it, ME! At that time, my father's parents did not have a phone, so my mother had to call his next-door neighbor who yelled down the street for him to come to the phone. Even though there was a separation between my parents, the news brought them back together, and soon after that, they purchased their first home. On November 12, 1981, I was born to happy parents and elated grandparents. All was going well, and in three years my younger sister was born.

After fourteen years of marriage, things were trying and challenging between my parents. Right before my sister started kindergarten, my mother decided to separate from my father. My mother packed up my younger sister and I and moved back in with her parents again. This would begin a difficult season for a single parent and me and my sister's childhood. The legal separation between my parents happened in 1988, but the divorce wasn't finalized until a year later, which was 1989. We eventually moved about twenty-five to thirty miles away from my grandparents, so my mother would be able to afford rent, which was $400 a month. We resided in that location for about 4 years before my mother was able to save enough money to purchase a home.

LONG ROAD AHEAD

Realization of rejection

Growing up, I don't think I paid attention to the fact that my father wasn't present. With him not being there for years, it seemed reasonable to me. My mom was always there and consistent, and that was the norm to me. When you don't know what normal is your reality sets the standard. Although my father wasn't around, it didn't erase the fact I knew I had one. I don't remember spending time with him or any meaningful conversations we had. What I do remember are times I wished he would come to pick me up and spend time with me. Unfortunately, that only happened in my imagination. There were many days that I longed for that, but it ended in utter disappointment.

As I got older, I felt the absence of my father. It wasn't until I became a grown man that I realized it. I was always quiet as a kid, most of that was due to my personality, although I believe some of it derived from isolation, and isolation from rejection. Because of my father's absence, I felt a sense of rejection. I think when a father leaves home and never returns, it's the gateway to abandonment and feelings of being unwanted for any kid. I often wondered why my father didn't want to see me, didn't want to pick me up and didn't want to take me places. What was wrong with me? What did I do to deserve that? My mind began to ask all types of questions and generate all kinds of answers and conclusions which were all wrong. The thought of not ever knowing the real answer led to years, even decades, of endless unanswered questions and false answers in my mind.

The rejection and abandonment I felt were traumatizing emotions. They are traumatizing to anyone, but I often think of the rejection and abandonment Jesus felt when God gave Him; His only begotten son to die for our sins. *"For God so loved the world that He gave His only begotten Son..." (John 3:16 NKJV).* Jesus dealt with rejection on some many levels. Not only did He experience it from God our Father but also from Judas and the people who did not believe He was the Messiah like the Pharisees. Like Jesus, I wished that my father would come to save me and fill the void of rejection and abandonment. *"O My Father, if it is possible, let this cup pass from Me; nevertheless, not as I will, but as You will"* (Matthew 26:39 NKJV). I'm not at all comparing myself to Jesus because His rejection was much more severe and on a different scale than my own, but I wanted to be saved. Saved from what at times, for a kid, felt like death but Jesus actually took on death. I went through a totally different situation, but I believe I experienced similar feelings, which is one of the reasons Jesus walked the earth, to take on the feelings and emotions of the flesh, a human.

Many scriptures note the emotions of Jesus. In Matthew 26:37-38, before Jesus was betrayed by Judas, Jesus states that he was sorrowful, distressed, and didn't want to be lonely. *"And He took with Him Peter and the two sons of Zebedee, and He began to be sorrowful and deeply distressed. Then He said to them, "My soul is exceedingly sorrowful, even to death. Stay here and watch with Me"* (Matthew 26:37-38 NKJV). This shows that we are not alone in having these feelings if our Savior had these feelings. I have felt horrible from rejection, abandonment, and loneliness, and I know many others have too. It's ok to have these feelings; it's just not ok to remain in those feelings. Later on in life, I learned that I was responsible for adequately dealing with the emotions I felt.

Most of my emotions were attached to this one question. "How can someone that should always be there for me, be the person that isn't there when I need them most?

Dealing with feelings of being unwanted is tough. Children aren't necessarily mature enough to process these feelings. I wasn't. Feeling rejected by others that include peers and friends is one thing, but when you experience it from a parent, that's on a different level.

Rejection can affect people differently. For me, rejection caused me to isolate myself from both of my parents. As a child, when you separate yourself from your parents, who do you talk to you? I didn't know how to deal with my emotions, so I kept them inside. As the years passed and I became older, I buried those feelings and emotions deeper and deeper inside. Those unspoken feelings resulted in me covering up the areas in me that were broken. Since I couldn't express it, I disguised it. I learned how to conceal so many things as a child. I masked my loneliness and unhappiness with a quiet demeanor. Not everyone handles their situation the same way. Some cry aloud with behaviors to attract attention. Both responses can be actions that hide the issues that individuals deal with internally. The longer I disguised my inner feelings, the deeper those feelings got buried, and the harder it was to heal from them. I wanted to appear strong and unbothered by those same circumstances that weakened me. I didn't want my feelings of rejection to have power over me, but the way I dealt with it gave rejection all the power. Rejection had power over me. For years I was powerless, fighting a battle that I could not win. The harder I fought it, the weaker I became because I was fighting it wrong. I avoided it instead of confronting it.

Loneliness accompanied the feelings of rejection and abandonment for me, and I found solitude to be worse than those feelings of rejection and abandonment. I felt there was no one there for me. I had no one to talk too. I didn't have a safety net, no one to help vet my rejection. I didn't know anything about casting my cares upon God. I Peter 5:7 asserts, *"Casting all your care upon Him, for He cares for you" (NKJV)*. I was at a place in my life where it felt like I had to deal with those experiences and feelings all alone.

The experiences started at such a young age. I didn't know how to communicate my feelings, nor was I taught to, so I kept them captive inside. I never learned to communicate well with my mother or anyone else for that matter. I mean, how do you talk to a mother that has a plate full of responsibilities and duties? One person can only be but so strong, and I knew she had so many feelings and emotions of her own to deal with. My mom did a fantastic job being a single mother, although many things fell through the cracks, including unspoken feelings and emotions.

I know my mother would have listened and addressed my concerns to the best of her ability, but she wasn't taught how to properly communicate her emotions either. Either way, rejection led me to isolate myself, which kept me from talking with my mother or anyone else. One way the enemy tries to restrict us is through isolation. Since I didn't know how to express myself and didn't have anyone to express myself to, I just kept to myself. What I thought was the best way to handle my pain was actually the enemy's plan to keep me isolated. Isolation doesn't necessarily mean that you are in a locked, dark bedroom by yourself. Isolation is being physically present in a room full of people but emotionally, mentally, and even spiritually distant. It occurs when you are burdened. You choose to keep your feelings and emotions within and dare to speak about them, and it causes you to remain quiet.

In keeping quiet, you miss out on the opportunity to be relational with other people who share your same experiences or have already been through it. The enemy doesn't want you in a relationship with someone who has experienced what you have and survived because their survival is the doorway to your survival and deliverance. That's exactly how the enemy works. He plans to make you feel rejected, so you isolate yourself. Nothing good happens when withdrawing from loved ones and community. Isolation will cause you to make poor decisions and life choices because you lack the individuals needed to give good counsel.

Plans fail for lack of counsel, but with many advisers, they succeed (Proverbs 15:22 NIV).

I had no idea the impact and effect my parents' divorce

would have on me, even at such a young age. Keeping my thoughts and feelings, concerning the divorce, inside affected me tremendously. I thought that I had no choice but to keep my feelings bottled up because I felt no one would listen. If they had the time to listen, what would they do about it? I felt that even if they had a solution, it wouldn't equal to what I really wanted, and that was the presence of my father. But truthfully the presence of only one father could fill my emptiness, and that was the presence of God the Father. *"My soul thirsts for God, for the living God. When shall I come and appear before God?" (Psalms 42:2 NKJV).*

The only problem was I didn't know God at that time. I was still trying to fill my void with earthly vessels and things.

"Do not lay up for yourselves treasures on earth, where moth and rust destroy and where thieves break in and steal; but lay up for yourselves treasures in heaven, where neither moth nor rust destroys and where thieves do not break in and steal. For where your treasure is, there your heart will be also" (Matthew 6:19-25 NKJV).

My heart was so set on receiving the love of a father. Not knowing that his love would always fail me just like every other person because we are all human. To replace that love, I looked for it in other places...

3

WRONG WAY

Mistaken Identity - Friendship

I grew up with something missing, a void that was never filled, and it caused me to search for what would. As a kid, I had several different "best friends." Friendships didn't last for whatever reason, there was always a disconnect. My lack of communication or inability to communicate was definitely a challenge for creating and sustaining friendships. As I remember it, I really didn't have much to talk about. Many would label it as being an introvert, which would be right about me, but I also think it came from years of suppression.

Short-lasting and invaluable friendships added to the insurmountable mountain of rejection I already had. I found myself asking, "What was wrong with me?" Because

I did not have friends or the ones I had, did not last long. I didn't have the answer to this question, so I started trying different ways to get and keep friends. I tried everything from the way I dressed to how I talked.

Later on in life, I realized God never intended for me to fit in and be friends with everyone. I was attempting to redesign myself to be accepted while negating God's intention for me. *"For You formed my inward parts; You covered me in my mother's womb" (Psalms 139:13 NKJV).* I was trying to change my personality, the way I thought and behaved; the very things that God made distinct about me. I did that or attempted to do those things to build and maintain relationships. Ironically, most of those relationships were with people that I was never intended to remain friends with, although I believe we were meant to be friends for that season. If I would have maintained or remained connected to some of those individuals, I may have never had the relationship with God that I do, know my purpose, reached my goals and/or strive for the destiny that God began to show me. I realized there was nothing wrong with me; in fact, I was unique for a reason. *"Before I formed you in the womb I knew you, before you were born, I set you apart" (Jeremiah 1:5 NKJV).* We have all been set apart. It is essential to acknowledge and embrace how God has set you apart. It's even more important to understand what it is that you do to set yourself apart. There is a difference between how

God sets you apart and what you do to set yourself apart...a life-changing difference.

My attempts to create and keep lasting friendships were because I hadn't learned who I was. My lack of identity caused me to adopt the character of those I was connected to. I was trying to be everyone but myself because I didn't know who John was.

Mistaken Identity – Alcoholism

Before sixteen, I was introduced to alcohol and began consuming it. It is prevalent in my family and bloodline. My environment was a factor in my drinking. At many of our family functions and events, there was beer and liquor present, and most of the men in my family drank. Although I had little to no contact with my father, I knew he drank and heard the allegations of him using other drugs. It was easy to become a product of my environment and fall in line with what the males in my family were doing. Of course, I didn't know it then, but I willingly became a part of the generational curse attached to my bloodline. The ignorance of myself and family opened the door for alcohol to become an idol. I can't count the number of times I turned to alcohol as a solution to life problems.

My cousins and I were used to seeing our uncles, and older cousins consume alcohol, so we began sneaking beers out of their coolers. One beer eventually led us, as underage drinkers, to wait outside of stores for adults, of age, to purchase beer and liquor for us. This went on for years until we were of age to buy it legally.

During my younger years, I never learned to value myself because I was always looking for someone else to love me. I was seeking love from my father the years he was absent, neglecting the opportunity to love myself. I didn't even know how to love myself. Since I was seeking the love of my father and never received it, I began to look everywhere else. At the start, alcohol seemed to produce the love that I desired. It gave me a community that had a common interest, which is what I lacked. It was a chance to hang with the fellas and be accepted. My friends and surrounding environments were always so inviting and welcoming to alcohol.

Alcohol not only gave me a community, but it also gave me social skills I never possessed. It allowed me to initiate and hold conversations I typically would not have and didn't have interest for. Alcohol gave me the reason to act out of character; a reason to be someone besides who I identified myself as. I could be a different person; a person that people would think was cool and fun to hang out with. It allowed me to put up a façade instead of learning and being my true self. It gave me a feeling of acceptance and courage. I had a boost of confidence, to most, known as liquid courage but liquid courage only lasts for the night or day, depending on when you started.

Most of the time, I was confident, accepted, and comfortable in environments that alcohol was present, but even if I wasn't, alcohol also gave me a nonchalant attitude and mentality. If I wasn't accepted, it didn't affect me as much. I believe that was what benefited me the most about drinking. I could live unapologetically. I didn't need to be accountable for my actions, what I said, any feelings that I had or the opinions and acceptance of people.

Drinking became something that I looked forward to, even at a young age. It became so entertaining, especially on the weekends when I would drink with my friends. Once we obtained our drink of choice for the night, we would just hang out and drink. Eventually, after enough alcohol was consumed, we'd find out where the party was which would mean, more liquor. The more liquor present meant a better party for me because alcohol aided my conversation with women. There wasn't a chick that I couldn't approach under the influence. The rejection was irrelevant when I was intoxicated. The enemy used the addiction to alcohol to cover the void rejection created. As mentioned earlier, being inebriated didn't last forever, so I frequently did it, or I did more of it to extend the moment. The more I drank, the longer I could make the moment last, so I did, and it became a lifestyle.

Mistaken Identity - Sex

As I began to mature and age, I continued to drink, and my interest in girls started to peak. Talking to the opposite sex was challenging, not because there wasn't a mutual interest, but because I was shy. Being the shy guy didn't really get me the pick of the litter. Girls had an interest in me, but to be honest, they weren't my first choices. It's entirely possible my first choices were out of my league, but over time, I noticed when I drank I was more inclined to approach girls I was more interested in. Drinking helped overcome the fear of initiating a conversation to more attractive girls. I could approach any girl while I was under the influence of alcohol. The conversation became natural and comfortable.

Of course, when I was drinking, I wasn't always thinking clearly. Honestly, I didn't want to. Drinking gave me the right to act loosely and not be accountable for my actions. I would make decisions under the influence that I would not usually make sober. More importantly, I was open season for attacks from the enemy. *"Be sober, be vigilant; because your adversary the devil walks about like a roaring lion, seeking whom he may devour"* (I Peter 5:8 NKJV). That is precisely what happened...

As a teenager, alcohol, pornography, and sex entered my life, all around the same time. Alcohol was definitely something I partook in every weekend and a few times during the week. Having sex was not as easily accessible as alcohol, but it happened often enough. If I didn't have a "girlfriend" or sexual partner, I would just masturbate to pornography or use my eidetic memory. I could always recall the image of an attractive female that I saw in person or on television.

It was always a good time whenever I was drunk or sexually active. I cannot deny that it was enjoyable and pleasurable almost all of the time. I loved to do it, and I looked forward to both. In the act of these things, I didn't really think much about it. Having sex and drinking was always great, but the feelings afterward weren't. I would feel guilt and shame almost immediately afterward.

It's like I knew I shouldn't be doing it, but it was pleasurable, even if it was temporary. Even after feeling remorseful, I would still continue to repeat those actions, moments later, the next day or night. I learned to alleviate guilt and shame by looking forward to the next time. One thing about sin is it never leaves you satisfied, it keeps you in a cycle, and the longer you're in the cycle, the harder it is to break. I was never satisfied by the last time I did it, so I was always looking for the next momentary, temporary fix. I wanted and needed more. I was never satisfied. I was in a cycle that I couldn't get out of, nor did I want to. *"And that they may come to their senses and escape the snare of the devil, having been taken captive by him to do his will" (2 Timothy 2:26 NKJV).* I was stuck in a permanent place doing temporary things. I knew I was in a snare and gripped by the stronghold of addiction and lust.

Mistaken Identity - Conflict with others

I didn't realize how deeply afflicted I became due to rejection. It affected how I dealt with resolving conflicts with others too. Instead of confronting conflict, I shied away from it. I avoided conflict. I was afraid of the rejection that could be a result of the conflict. The possibility that I would be the cause of someone wanting to discount being acquainted with me was fearful. I was less concerned about losing a friend and more concerned about what others thought of me. Avoiding the conflict was a defense mechanism to eliminate knowing the thoughts they had of me. It's funny how what I used to avoid is what I now encourage. What if they were actually right and I didn't do something the right way? Shouldn't I know that? Not to know the opinions of others of me but for possible betterment of myself. I learned that criticism is useful, especially if it's constructive and from trusted, reliable sources. When you operate from a place of independence and pride, everything you do is right, and there is no other way. Most of the time, that is not true. We rob ourselves of the opportunity to grow when we limit the voices in our lives that could help us change. Constructive criticism was hard for me to accept because I never received it or was open to it.

Not only was constructive criticism or feedback hard to receive, but it was hard to receive from those close to me. Those closest to you are the ones you should be most willing to gain from. Who is better to receive feedback and advice from than those who know you intimately? They observe you carefully and can widen the perspective of your narrow view.

When we're not secure in our identity, it's difficult to receive constructive criticism. It's difficult because we don't receive it as constructive but as destructive. The actual knowledge of self helps us put our guard down and keep us from being defensive about what is said that may benefit us.

Maintaining relationships is an area that I still tend to struggle in. Over the years, I've seen friends come and go. A lot of it came from how I grew up. At a young age, I learned how to care for myself. I never depended on anyone. After a certain age, I didn't even depend on my mother. If I needed something or needed to do something, I would do it on my own. I adopted the mentality that I could do life for myself, by myself. By doing this, I squandered the importance and chance to build strong and lasting relationships. I didn't know how to value relationships because I didn't have great examples of relationship in my life, nor had I observed the significance of them.

Growing up, my mother didn't really have friends because she was too busy raising my sister and I, working and going to school, so extra time for a social life was scarce. The only relationships I observed her having was with family and church family. To me, it only seemed like surface relationships; nothing too deep or intimate. Her relationships were not because of wanting or desire but more of necessity from my viewpoint. Most of family time would involve sitting around and talking about surface issues and laughing at the jokes my uncles and cousins would tell. I didn't witness a conversation or interaction where someone was really opening up about how they felt or what they were going through. If I did, it was few and far between. It was kind of an unwritten, unspoken thing. It just didn't happen in my family or in my surroundings, especially between men.

The men in my family rarely talked about feelings. Conversations, for the most part, included sports, women, drinking, cars, etc. Opening up about feelings amongst men usually led to an awkward silence or a joke to blow it off. I'm sure in most black families, it is just an uncomfortable conversation for men and somehow in our minds diminishes our masculinity. It's usually not an atmosphere conducive for open dialogue about feelings. That was often what the women did while they were in the house, separate from the men.

4

TAKE A STEP

I believe it was a Friday night when I received a call from a cousin on my father's side. She told me that my father had a stroke and that the doctors were not expecting him to live. Since I did not have a relationship with him, and he was like a stranger, I didn't have any feelings about the situation. If I'm brutally honest, I did not care if he lived or died. His existence or non-existence did not affect my life one way or the other. I was numb to the fact that the only biological father that I would ever have was about to die. The call ended, and I never thought any more about the situation.

Within a week, I got another call. This call was to inform me that my father did not die from his stroke, as they had previously presumed, but instead was in a coma.

My response was, "Ok, ...well good for him." Although those were my true and initial feelings, my feelings began to change. I felt God begin to soften my heart towards my father and the situation. I began to be burdened with mishandling the situation. Over the next few days, God began to deal with me unusually. The spirit of forgiveness filled my heart. I had no clue where these feelings came from, the only explanation was God. I was initially ok with my father dying if it were to happen. It sounds cruel, but it's true. It wouldn't have been a loss to or for me. There wasn't an emotional, physical, or spiritual connection to him for over twenty-five years, so there was nothing for me to miss.

I was hesitant to forgive him, but God laid it on my heart so heavy that I really didn't have a choice. So after fighting myself and God, I limped away like Jacob with a different heart posture. Although I didn't want to forgive my father, there was a tug in my spirit to do so. Going into the situation, I felt like I was limping. I had no idea what to do or how to do it. I felt handicapped, and the outcome of what would happen was so unpredictable.

My father was in a hospital near Fort Washington, PA. It was about three or more hours from where I was currently living in Gaithersburg, Maryland. After vacillating with the idea all week, one Saturday, I took the three hour drive to see my father. I didn't know what to expect when I got there. I didn't know if he was conscious or unconscious, if he would recognize me or not...all I knew is that God laid it on my heart to do this, so I did. When I arrived, my father was still in a coma, unconscious. As I was there, a level of compassion came over me. To see anyone in that condition causes you to have empathy. How could I not have those sentiments for my own father? To see him fighting for his life was not something that I would wish on anyone. As far as I knew, he could not hear or see anything. Tubes were connected to him coming, both, in and out. The only thing I knew to do at that time was to pray. I didn't pray down heaven or anything like that, but there was something special about it. Now that I look back on it, I believe that was the moment that changed both of our lives. Have you ever had the feeling that something was happening, but you didn't really know what? That's how I felt at that moment of prayer. I don't have words or language to express how I felt or what was happening, but I did indeed feel a shift. I was only there for about twenty minutes, but I felt such an impactful move of God in a short period. After I prayed, I left and drove back home with a million and one thoughts running through my mind and a heavier heart.

Over the next few weeks and months, I battled feelings that I didn't have to before. After years of ill feelings towards my father, now I actually cared that he was dying. Despite the ill feelings I had, I was now pulling for him to gain his consciousness back...and he did! I believe that prayer was one of the things or possibly the only thing that brought life back into his body. Prayer works! I don't know for a fact that my prayer is what saved his life, but suppose it was. If I allowed the hardness of my heart to keep me from praying for him, what would have happened? I received word he came out of his coma, and he was conscious. As I was silently cheering on his recovery, I began to think about what was next. I never thought about whether I would go see him if he came out of his coma? I struggled with this question for a while. As before God laid it so heavy on my heart that I had no choice.

My father was moved from the hospital to a rehabilitation center that was close to it, so I decided to take the drive up there. That three-hour drive was nerve-wracking, to say the least. My thoughts were all over the place; I mean, what would I say? What if I didn't recognize him? Even worse, what if he didn't remember me? I prayed and spoke to God about it the entire ride. Every time my anxieties got the best of me, He would comfort me. *"Fear not, for I am with you; Be not dismayed, for I am your God. I will strengthen you, Yes, I will help you, I will uphold you with My righteous right hand"* (Isaiah 41:10 NKJV). Unconsciously aware, I would let my anxieties get the best of me over and over again during the drive. The drive was definitely a roller-coaster ride for me. I finally arrived at the rehabilitation center. I turned off the car and sat there. After driving three hours, I still contemplated whether I should even go into that rehabilitation center. Crazy, right? Fear started to overcome me, stronger than it had the whole car ride. I questioned myself and asked, what was the point of going to see him now after so many years? After five to ten minutes of sitting in the car and thinking about how the situation would play out, I did the only thing I knew to do...I prayed! I prayed that God would help me take authority of my fear and that He would go before me and that His will would be done.

"Hear my prayer, O LORD, and let my cry come to You. Do not hide Your face from me in the day of my trouble; incline Your ear to me; in the day that I call, answer me speedily" (Psalms 102:17 NKJV).

As soon as my prayer was over, I got out of my car and walked into the rehab center. I walked in and went to the receptionist and told them my father's name, and they gave me his room number. I proceeded to walk to his room, ready for whatever was going to take place. When I walked into the room, no one was there. I remembered seeing a community room by the receptionist desk where there were residents gathered eating lunch. I peeked in the room, and there were only two or three black men in there, and none of them looked like my father. I kindly walked up to the receptionist desk again and said that my father was not in his room and asked if they knew where he was. The receptionist said, "Are you his son?" and I responded, "yes."

She said, "I knew it, you look just like him." She then said that he was in the community room having lunch, and I said you must be mistaken because I didn't see him. She got out of her chair and walked to the community room, and I followed her. Then she pointed to him and said there he is. She told me I could go in there and sit with him. I told her that it was ok and that I would wait for him to finish. I immediately walked out of the rehab center and stood outside.

The reason that I didn't want to go in there wasn't so that he could finish lunch but because I had so many mixed feelings that started to come over me. For one, he looked so different. He had lost so much weight. I didn't even recognize him. I thought I was ready to confront my fears, the bitterness, the resentment, the rejection, the hatred, and the years of abandonment, but I wasn't. While standing outside, I had to arrest my emotions and get them under control. I still don't know what made me emotional the most. Was it his frail body, how he looked which was completely different than what I remembered him, or the fact that I was about to sit down and have a conversation with him for the first time in over two decades?

Once again, I had to rely on God. I uttered a short prayer, and He quickly assured me I was doing the right thing, and there was nothing to fear. *"For God has not given us a spirit of fear, but of power and of love and of sound mind"* (2 Timothy 1:7 NKJV). I proceeded back inside the rehab center and walked into the community room. I gently placed my hand on the back of his shoulder as he looked up from his plate and I said, "Hey man, how you doing?" As he gave me a confused look, he said, "Good." I responded by telling him that I would be in his room after he finished his lunch, and he said, "ok."

As I walked out, I felt a slight sense of relief. I took the first step, which felt like a momentous first leap. I sat in the room and patiently waited. Strangely enough, the feelings that I felt earlier no longer existed. I sat in that chair fearless and ready for what was next. As he came rolling into the room in his wheelchair, I felt reasonably confident. I asked him how his meal was, and he replied that was it was good. Then he asked a question that almost floored me. He said, "Now, who are you again?" At that very moment, I wanted to walk out and never go back again. I was utterly taken back by the question. That question pretty much dug up every thought that I had over the past twenty-five years and during that three-hour car ride that I tried to get rid of. All the abandonment, rejection, and resentment came over me all at once. As there was a slight pause, I didn't really know what was going to happen next. After what felt like a long hesitation, I spoke and said, "You don't know who I am?" The lady at the front desk said that I look just like you." Still unsure, he said... "JW"... and I said, "Yeah, it's me." With a look of both excitement and unbelief, he said, "Hey." From there, we began to converse.

As the conversation developed, it was actually pretty cool to sit and talk with him. After the initial awkwardness, in the beginning, all seemed to go well. He even ended up asking me to cut his hair, which was unexpected. After we finished talking, I prayed for him and left. As I was walking to my car, I didn't really know what to feel. My emotions and feelings were somewhat all over the place and mixed. I had a good three-hour drive to process everything that happened, but one of the first things I did was thank God for laying forgiveness on my heart and comforting me as I went through with it.

One important thing that I learned during that interaction was I kept pressing through, even though at times I didn't want to. *"Not that I have already attained, or am already perfected; but I press on, that I may lay hold of that for which Christ Jesus has also laid hold of me. Brethren, I do not count myself to have apprehended; but one thing I do, forgetting those things which are behind and reaching forward to those things which are ahead, I press toward the goal for the prize of the upward call of God in Christ Jesus" (Philippians 3:12-14 NKJV).*

This scripture became the theme for my life and helped push me through every feeling that opposed forgiveness and overcoming hard times. There were times where I wanted to give up and just go home, but what God placed in me and what He needed me to accomplish on that day, wouldn't let me give in. Of course, it was hard, challenging, and pushed me far outside of my comfort zone, but the reward was everything. I didn't really begin to experience the reward right away. As I was processing my thoughts and all that transpired, I realized that I experienced deliverance from unforgiveness. Although a residue still remained, I believe that I was freed. It felt like a weight and burden was lifted off of me.

5

PAY THE TOLL

O vercoming fatherlessness is a daunting task by itself. Forgiving the person that left you fatherless is out of the question for most and unfortunately never happens. As simple as it might sound, I believe it is because people don't know that they should forgive or how to forgive. Some tools and steps can be taken to make this intimidating assignment achievable. Here are six steps that I think would help anyone forgive.

Having a covenant relationship with God

Sounds like a simple step but having a relationship with God is not as simple as saying you have one and check it off the list. A relationship with God is a daily walk. It is seeking Him with a submitted heart and mind to do His will. When you have a relationship with God, it makes you want to do the right thing, no matter how hard it is. You want to live right by Him and people. No matter how long you run from it, the weight of doing life God's way will eventually wear you down. The whole process of forgiving my father started with God placing a burden on my heart that would not go away. A relationship with God puts an expectation on you to do the will of God, regardless of what someone has done to you or how you feel about doing it. The deeper your relationship with God is, the more you feel the need to change your past behaviors and thought processes. That includes forgiving and loving a person that has wronged you. Not only that, but to do it over and over again. "Lord, how many times will my brother sin against me, and I forgive him and let it go? Up to seven times?" Jesus answered him, *"I say to you, not up to seven times, but seventy times seven" (Matthew 18:21-22 AMP).*

Hearing from God

A relationship with God is daily, open, flowing communication between you and Him. God doesn't speak to us with one form of communication. God speaks to us through our prayers, reading the Bible, in praise and worship, through other people, visions and dreams, etc. God can speak to us in various ways. For example, God opened the mouth of a donkey to speak to Balaam and opened Balaam's eyes that he may see the Angel of the Lord and hear Him.

"And the LORD *opened the mouth of the donkey, and she said to Balaam, "What have I done to you that you have struck me these three times?" "The Angel of the* LORD *said to him, "Why have you struck your donkey these three times? Behold, I have come out to stand against you because your behavior was obstinate and contrary to Me." (Numbers 22:28, 32 AMP).*

God, without question, speaks! Are we open to receiving it is the question?

I would not have forgiven my father if I did not hear from God. Forgiving my father was not a desire of mine, but a conviction from God, and I couldn't ignore what God was saying. God put such a burden on me that I had to respond. I was convicted by Him. I faithfully and intentionally listened for the voice of God during the entire process. In the beginning, I heard Him say to forgive. During the process, when I began to talk myself out of it, He assured me I was capable. Afterward, I felt the burden lifted off and the affirmation from God. *"...Well done, good and faithful servant..." (Matthew 25:23 NKJV).*

Hearing and conversing with God is not like speaking with another human being, for most of us. God can talk to you and me totally different. It's imperative that you find out the many ways God speaks and how God is speaking to

you. Be diligent about hearing the voice of God and what
He is saying.

All of us hear from God. *"My sheep hear My voice, and I
know them, and they follow Me" (John 10:27 NKJV).* Never
question whether you hear from God, but whether you are
in the posture to hear. His sheep not only hear, but they
follow Him, meaning they obey his voice and command-
ments. Hearing is not just listening but doing.

> *"Don't fool yourself into thinking that you are a listener when
> you are anything but, letting the Word go in one ear and out the
> other. Act on what you hear! Those who hear and don't act are
> like those who glance in the mirror, walk away, and two minutes
> later have no idea who they are, what they look like" (James 1:22
> MSG).*

Forgiveness is for you, your health, and well-being

The truth of the matter is unforgiveness is a heavy weight
to bear. I was tired of carrying around the weight and
burden of unforgiveness, anger, bitterness, and resentment.
There is a famous quote, written a couple of different ways
that explains what unforgiveness does to us. "Unforgiveness is like drinking poison waiting for the other person to
die." Unforgiveness affects us more than it does the
person(s) we are holding a grudge against. Most of us, at
least at one time or another, have used being mad or angry

at someone as an excuse to not speak to them, hold a grudge, or to get back at them. Falsely believing that not talking to them or holding a grudge against them would somehow reciprocate the hurt we feel. We don't realize how much more we are actually hurting ourselves. More times than not, the person we are trying to hurt is enjoying life while we are still carrying the offense. We put so much energy and effort indirectly trying to hurt them, we don't recognize that we're the one suffering. The energy you put into it is draining. It leaves us physically, mentally, emotionally, and most importantly, spiritually fatigue. You have to want to forgive for yourself, for your own well-being. *"A merry heart does good like medicine, but a broken spirit dries the bones" (Proverbs 17:22 NKJV).*

Don't let forgiveness deplete you of life

In a study, Charlotte vanOyen Witvliet, a psychologist at Hope College, asked people to think about someone who had hurt, mistreated, or offended them. While they thought about this person and their past offense, she monitored their blood pressure, heart rate, facial muscle tension, and sweat gland activity. To ruminate on an old situation with hurt can indicate unforgiveness. Sure enough, in Witvliet's research, when people recalled a grudge, their physical arousal soared. Their blood pressure and heart rate increased, and they sweated more. Ruminating about their grudges was stressful, and subjects found the rumination unpleasant. It made them feel angry, sad, anxious, and less in control. Witvliet also asked her subjects to try to empathize with their offenders or imagine forgiving them. When they practiced forgiveness, their physical arousal coasted downward. They showed no more of a stress reaction than normal wakefulness produces. (The New Science of Forgiveness, Everett L. Worthington Jr., Greater Good Magazine, www.greatergood.berkeley.edu).

My first observation was how easily we can recall the person and the past hurt, mistreatment, and offense we associate with them. Secondly, the behavior of people who still harbor unforgiveness. We are not necessarily called to forget, but we are called to forgive. Many of us do the opposite, we forget and don't forgive, or we think we have forgotten it, but really we have just suppressed it. This quickly causes what we have temporarily suppressed to surface by triggers or the mention of the past circumstance. Just because you can remember the events of hurt, mistreatment, and offense doesn't mean those offended feelings should still be attached to them. When you have forgiven, you should be able to remember the incidents and the lessons learned without the ill feelings that were once associated with it.

It's also interesting how the thought of the hurt, mistreatment, or offense puts unwarranted pressure on the body of those affected. *"A calm and peaceful and tranquil heart is life and health to the body" (Proverbs 14.30 AMP)*. If a calm, peaceful, and tranquil heart is life and health, then a heart that harbors unforgiveness, resentment and bitterness cannot be at peace and is poor health, which leads to death. Of course, it doesn't mean that you'll die immediately, but slowly your health and life will deteriorate.

"Do not be wise in your own eyes; Fear the Lord [with reverent awe and obedience] and turn [entirely] away from evil. It will be health to your body [your marrow, your nerves, your sinews, your muscles—all your inner parts] And refreshment (physical well-being) to your bones" (Proverbs 3:7-8 AMP).

Again, if fearing the Lord and turning away from evil is healing to your flesh and refreshment to your bones then carrying unforgiveness which is not fearing the Lord, because the will of the Lord is forgiveness, is sickening to the flesh and decaying to the bones.

Don't talk yourself out of it

What's important to understand about forgiveness is that it's a decision. The act of forgiveness is a decision, but I believe healing from unforgiveness is a process. It's not easy and does not happen right away. When I decided that I was going to forgive my father, every feeling that I had about him, and my situation didn't go away instantly. As I stated earlier, I vacillated about making the decision to forgive him. I knew I needed to do it and why, but at other times I could think of every reason why I didn't want to or why I shouldn't do it. Every reason from, he is the father, he should do it, to what difference will it make.

There were several reasons why I shouldn't forgive him, and they outweighed the reasons why I should. There was one reason that I couldn't overlook, and it outweighed all the others...God. It wasn't about the number of reasons but the significance in the reasons that made the difference. My freedom, deliverance, and purpose depended on it, and those things are worth way more than the bitterness and resentment that I held on to for decades, plus I love God!

There will be several times when you are discouraged or influenced not to forgive. The world we live in will have you believe unforgiveness is the right thing to do. In a time where beef, quarrels, and grudges in politics and entertainment are common, we are still called to be righteous.

"Don't copy the behavior and customs of this world, but let God transform you into a new person by changing the way you think."
(Romans 12:2 NLT).

There is always a fight between what you see in the natural and what you know in your spirit. Your flesh will always try to overpower your spirit.

"For the sinful nature has its desire which is opposed to the Spirit, and the [desire of the] Spirit opposes the sinful nature; for these [two, the sinful nature and the Spirit] are in direct opposition to each other [continually in conflict], so that you [as believers] do not [always] do whatever [good things] you want to do" (Galatians 5:17 AMP).

You have to fight against the opposition of the flesh. The opposition will even cause you to stall, avoid and delay making the decision to forgive, giving ground to the enemy to use your indecisiveness as a playground and now your offense has turned into a cycle instead of a confrontation. One circumstance has now become a lifestyle. The longer we delay forgiveness, the harder it is, and it becomes normal for how we handle offenses.

Don't talk yourself out it. Confront your offense head on. Identify what the offense is, understand why you're offended, release your offender, acknowledge what you want to communicate to your offender and set a deadline as to when you want to confront it, then face it – sooner than later. Break the cycle before it starts.

Maintaining freedom

Another critical component of forgiveness is maintaining freedom from unforgiveness. Unfortunately, just because you received freedom from unforgiveness does not mean that you'll never have to deal with it again. In fact, there will be times where the very offense that you forgave will come back to your remembrance.

There are two things, I believe need to take place when this occurs:

Pray that the fire of God consumes and burns every negative thought, not like Him and that did not come from Him.

Bring those thoughts into captivity to the obedience of Christ (2 Corinthians 10:5 NKJV). You have to renew your mind and remind yourself that those thoughts are not from God and not the will of God. Instead of being a prisoner to those thoughts, bring those thoughts into the imprisonment of a Christ-like mind.

I know...I can count! Here's a bonus! Remember that your freedom is much more crucial. You fought too hard to get free, so don't give away your freedom that easy.

If you don't have to deal with the remembrance or flare-up of an old offense, you may be tested with a similar offense or an offense at a higher, more intimate level.

"Now, when the unclean spirit has gone out of a man, it roams through waterless (dry, arid) places in search of rest, but it does not find it. Then it says, 'I will return to my house from which I came.' And when it arrives, it finds the place unoccupied, swept, and put in order. Then it goes and brings with it seven other spirits more wicked than itself, and they go in and make their

home there. And the last condition of that man becomes worse than the first" (Matthew 12:45 AMP).

Once you've been freed from the offense, it's essential to maintain that freedom. You maintain it by living a Godly lifestyle by daily prayer, covering yourself in the full armor of God. It is easy to allow yourself to return to old habits, ways, and mindsets, but you must acknowledge the good in your decision and the steps you have made. It is essential to submit yourself to God, be a reader and doer of the word, and pray without ceasing. When you remain in a posture submitted to God, it reminds you why you forgave past offenses and keeps you from staying in offense and falling into new offenses.

Your deliverance and freedom are going to take a fight from you, and that involves you denying your flesh by taking captive every thought that comes against keeping your freedom. You can be assured that the areas of your life that you were offended in will be tested again. The sooner you are aware of the testing, the sooner you can put your thoughts and actions into the proper perspective. Acknowledging the test at the occurrence of it keeps it from growing into offense and allows you to war against it in prayer and the word of God.

You must remain guarded and have on the full armor of God. Whenever you allow unforgiveness or any sin to enter, it opens the doorway and entry point for other sins.

You must avoid that from happening, even if you initially miss the mark, repent, and do it no more. The word says, *"If we confess our sins, He is faithful and just to forgive us our sins and to cleanse us from all unrighteousness"* (1 John 1:9 NKJV). Just because you fell into sin, doesn't mean you have to stay there. Don't let the enemy use your sin against you! He is famous for using your sin as an opportunity to lay the weight of stubbornness and pride, along with guilt, shame, and condemnation.

Pride and stubbornness will keep you from confronting the sin or offense, but guilt, shame, and condemnation will make you magnify your imperfections and devalue yourself. You pay the price for your sins that were already paid for when Jesus died on the cross. *"There is therefore now no condemnation to those who are in Christ Jesus"* (Romans 8:1 NKJV). Your sin does not disqualify you from your purpose or from who God has called you to be. Your purpose does not become void because of what you've done.

"For the gifts and the calling of God are irrevocable [for He does not withdraw what He has given, nor does He change His mind about those to whom He gives His grace or to whom He sends His call]" (Romans 11:29 KJV).

It's the gateway to your purpose

One night I was feeling depressed and felt like my life was purposeless. Life felt like I was just going through the motions. There was a void. I had no purpose, at least that's how I felt. I didn't have any promises or goals that I was working towards. I wasn't sure what I was born to do.

As I was in bed, thinking about the process of forgiving my father, tears began to saturate my pillow because honestly, I knew it was healing for me. I knew life wouldn't progress for me without forgiving him. As those tears continued to pour, and I began to cry out and talk to God. He began to reveal the purpose of my last twenty-five years. As God spoke, I heard Him with more clarity than I had ever heard Him before. He clearly showed me that what I went through was just preparation for me. He showed me how my fatherlessness gave me a passion for the fatherless and a father's heart for them. Part of my purpose would be to help others who have dealt and are dealing with the same childhood and adult challenges, particularly males, young and old. He was going to use the very thing that I struggled with to be part of my purpose and a passion for the rest of my life. He was going to use the same thing that was a burden to be a blessing, as he often does.

More often than not, God uses the burdens we have struggled with, to be a testimony to bless those who are currently going through it. *"But I have prayed for you, that your faith should not fail; and when you have returned to Me, strengthen your brethren" (Luke 22:32 NKJV).* God knows that our faith gets weak at times. What a blessing it is to serve a God that prays that our faith will not fail, no matter what situation or circumstance we are in. Not only that, but He is confident that we will get through it because He says, "When you have returned to Me." That means that our weakness of faith is temporary. Our feelings are temporary. Our emotions are temporary. Our situation is temporary! What a blessing that God knows that we'll return to Him and that He'll use what made us weak as strength for us and our brethren.

After that night, God began to use me in exactly what He showed me. Before I knew it, I was coaching a youth basketball team with my church's sports ministry. I enjoyed basketball but never saw myself coaching again. To be honest, I thought I was horrible at it. The team I was coaching, years prior, lost every game! If I was really supposed to be coaching and was any good at it, then I should have at least won one game! I realized that I had absolutely no clue what I was doing out there, and it was harder than I thought it was. My competitiveness wouldn't let me see beyond wins and losses at the time, but I was looking at it all wrong. I was looking at it naturally and not spiritually. My responsibility and role was not to be the most winningest coach in recreational basketball history or to even win a game that season. I was placed there to learn my purpose, to be a role model, to be a mentor! Because I didn't fully know my purpose, I couldn't adequately fulfill it. So I wasn't the most winningest coach in rec ball history, and I wasn't the best mentor/role model I could be either. I'm not saying I didn't have a positive influence on the kids, but I could have had a greater impact if I realized my purpose for being there.

In 2016, the opportunity presented itself again. The young men on my team ranged from 13-15 years old. Immediately, I saw the impact that I would make on some of these young men's lives. Of course, I love the sport of basketball and wanted to win, but this time, I knew my assignment was about more than basketball. Basketball was just being used as a means for my purpose to manifest. I began to establish relationships with these young men, mostly from being their transportation and our interactions during practice and games. To be honest, providing rides in the past would have been a little irritating. That's one of the ways, I knew I was in my purpose, and it was the right timing. Nothing bothered me about coaching the basketball team (except losing of course and I could have done without the bald jokes). I enjoyed it and looked forward to every practice, game, and every ride. I loved the fact that I was a positive role model in their lives, and some of their mothers were too.

Even after moving more than 10 hours away, I still keep in contact with some of the players and their families. It's good to know that they are doing well and that I possibly played a part in that, even if it was a small one.

God wasn't done there. While serving in a ministry at church, I met a good friend who shared the same passion and purpose I did towards the fatherless. As we talked about it, we shared our interest in starting a non-profit organization dedicated to fatherless youth. We along with another young lady put in the work, shared thoughts and ideas, and began to plan the launch of our nonprofit focused on fatherless young ladies, "Heart of a Father" in August 2016. We put hard work into the organization hoping to one day make a difference in the lives of young ladies with absent fathers, anticipating the expansion of it to young men. Eventually, in spring 2017, we were invited to test our curriculum and program at a high school in the District of Columbia. We were able to have three successful sessions before the school year ended that were impactful and promising. The young ladies involved were very active and provided excellent dialogue and feedback. We were definitely on the right path and on the verge of creating something great.

Unfortunately, God had other plans. In May 2017, I was presented with a promotion on my job that required me to relocate. When I was initially presented with the opportunity by my supervisor, I informed him that I didn't think the position was for me and that I wasn't interested in relocating. Life was really going well for me. My supervisor told me to think about it over the weekend and to call the regional controller that I would possibly work for on Monday. I agreed to at least do that.

I felt the need to begin a fast, so immediately I did. It was strange to me that my supervisor told me to think about a promotion over the weekend after I basically declined it. After fasting, praying, and receiving several confirmations, it was God's will for me to accept the position and relocate to Atlanta. That meant leaving the basketball team I coached and all the work that was done for the nonprofit. The decision made me bittersweet, but I knew it was what I had to do.

6

SCENIC ROUTE

One day a friend, Richard texted me and it started out as a normal, regular text thread. Out of nowhere, the thread shifted. We started texting about his father. He mentioned the difficulty of getting close to his father and the reasons why he thought that was. Richard told his father that he had forgiven him for the past and that they needed to move on. He had forgiven his father for the way he treated his mother over the years. Acts of infidelity and having several kids by different women definitely caused division within the family. After all those years, my friend was able to forgive his father. Richard's father felt like the children held a grudge against him and disliked him, which made his father dismiss the attempt of connecting with his children.

My friend was confused over his father's perspective because, after all those years, he had never sat him or his siblings down to have that conversation with them. I'm sure a lot of fatherless sons and daughters have thought that at some point. I responded to my friend with a word of encouragement. I assured him that forgiving my father was the biggest thing I did in my life. I explained to him how I thank God, He gave me the strength to do it. I always thought he as the father (my father) should do it, but God showed me how the responsibility was on me, and I had to do it. God basically showed me how I had to mature and take on the role I thought my father should have. The response my friend gave me was absolutely unexpected, but I needed to see it. He said, "And you did, I applaud you. I've seen it. That's why I'm stepping to him now." That response blew me away for two reasons. One – I didn't know that anyone paid enough attention to notice that I forgave my father and reconciled with him. Two – It never truly dawned on me that my obedience to God would be used as an example to encourage someone else.

While conversing with another friend, we discussed our history and the relationships that we had with our fathers. He was describing how his relationship with his father was good now, but it wasn't always that way. His relationship with his father was ruined by his drug use and by infidelity. He reminisced on how his father left his mother for another woman. He didn't realize what was happening but would go to the other woman's house just to be connected with his father. As he got older and realized what happened, the relationship between the two became non-existent. My question to him was, how were you able to build a relationship with him after all of that? He said that he didn't become connected with his father until he saw him connected to the Father (God).

Our alignment and connection with God should be the perfect example of how the relationship between father and son should be. How are children to learn what authority is and how it looks, if their parents are not submitted to authority? Your relationship with God should be an example to others, particularly non-believers, and it should encourage others to desire a relationship with God too. It's hard to convert non-believers when your relationship with God consists of a bad attitude, always complaining, behaviors that don't line up with the word of God, and you resist to submitting to the authority of God. Our relationships with people are an indication of where our relationship is with God. If you're not loyal and loving to your friends and others, how does that reflect in your relationship with Christ?

"A new commandment I give unto you, that ye love one another; as I have loved you, that ye also love one another. By this shall

all men know that ye are my disciples if ye have love one to another" (John 13:34-35, NKJV).

Our love for others is a demonstration of our love for Him.

7

PIT STOPS

According to the National Center for Fathering, 20 million children are impacted by absent fathers in the home. 57.6% of black children are living absent their biological fathers (Family Structure and Children's Living Arrangements 2012, Vespa, Jonathan, Lewis, Jamie and Kreider, Rose, https://www.census.gov/prod/2013pubs/p20-570.pdf). One can only wonder what effect does this have on children and families, particularly in the black community. I heard a question asked on a radio show that engrossed me. The question was, "Are mothers protecting and coddling their sons too much in the absence of fathers?" The questions continued as another asked, "Have young black boys and teenagers been deceived as what a man is and how to represent one?" Since young males are spending the majority of their time with their mother, what habits and mannerisms are they developing, and which are they lacking with the father being absent? In a household where the mother is a single parent, young men witness their mothers providing for the home, which could diminish the leadership role that they should have as a man.

Another opinion that was made during the radio show was that single mothers are treating their sons as their dates or as they would a boyfriend by calling their sons bae or boo. Mothers are replacing a mate or significant other with their sons, and once they gain companionship, the son is left reliving the familiar feelings of abandonment that they experienced with their father.

Most of these actions taken by single mothers have lasting effects that mothers are unconsciously aware of, as well as fathers. Understandably so, there is not a blueprint or manual on how to raise children in a two-parent household, let alone a single parent household. So as always, the question remains, how do we resolve these type of issues?

I believe the beginning starts with bringing these issues to the forefront. There cannot be a resolution or an answer to a problem when it is ignored and treated as normal. It seems as though the community continues to sweep these underlying issues under the rug and other issues take precedence over it. No one wants to talk about it, resulting in the increasing number of young men without the guidance, direction, upbringing, and the definition of identity needed. We then assume we can correct the years of the void by placing them around responsible men in the church, mentorship programs or activities. I'm definitely in favor of mentorship programs but are they effective if the child's identity remains an issue? These programs can't be used, just solely, to place the young men around positive role models and men but to attack the root and reaffirm their identity.

8

WHAT DOES IT COST?

I've seen and heard many stories of the effect of abandonment and rejection and the mark left on individuals, and it's disheartening. A friend told me how most of her life she didn't know her father and described the effect it had on her. Even after she connected with her father, he displayed favoritism to a sibling that he had known longer than her. Although I feel there is never a valid reason or excuse for the absence of a father, I do wonder what causes a father to adopt such actions. What makes them feel they don't need to be involved in their child's life, especially after missing so much of it already? Often times, we view other's lives and situations and vow that we would never do what they are doing, but do we honestly know what we would do if we were placed in that circumstance? *"Judge not, that you be not judged. For with what judgment you judge, you will be judged; and with the measure you use, it will be measured back to you"* (Matthew 7:1-2, NKJV). Each of us can look back on life and point out at least one circumstance or situation where we can honestly say that we never imagined that we would have reacted like that.

I've learned that we tend to look at our present situations and circumstances through the lenses of our past. It's all about how we view ourselves. Guilt, shame, and condemnation often leave us in the very posture that we pray to get out of. I wonder if along with these things, self-worth keeps a father absent from their earthly creation. Why does a father abandon their child(ren) or decide to play a minimal part in their lives? This, to me, is a fundamental question that we have avoided, and I believe that the answers to this question from absent fathers could help break the spirit of fatherlessness and the cycle of broken families. When I forgave my father, I also lost the desire to know what the reason for my abandonment was. After my father suffered his stroke, dementia began to set in. If I asked, I'm not sure if I would get an answer and if I did, would it be a satisfying and honest answer? It didn't dawn on me until I started writing this book that I never got an answer and really don't need one.

Who would be better to ask about fatherlessness but

absent fathers? If we were able to have a no judgment zone where absent fathers could talk about the reasoning behind the abandonment of their children, maybe there would be a better understanding of the issues and challenges that have prevented these men from being upstanding and outstanding fathers.

I believe if most absent fathers would share their reasons, the answers would probably be the same or very similar. In listening to a video from Oprah's Life Class on "Absent Fathers," an absent dad explained why men leave their children and why he left his wife and children. He said,

"I left because at the moment I wasn't the man I wanted to be for them. One thing led to another, and I went from marijuana to alcohol. I put them on a higher pedestal than I put myself. There was a point when I felt I wasn't worthy of being in their lives because I wasn't the man that I would want for them."

Roland Warren of The National Fatherhood Initiative said, "Good fathers do three things: provide, nurture and guide. Yet, too many men have warped ideas of what this means, and it sets them up for feeling unworthy. The 'provide' part, a lot of times, guys will make that economics," "But it's not just about presents... but presence. Warren continued by saying, "You create this script of what this ideal father is supposed to be, and then you try to live up to a script that's not reality... And then when you don't [live up to it], you feel, 'I'm not worthy,' and you pull away." Iyanla Vanzant went on to say, "I have found [that] the kryptonite for men is inadequacy."

Most absent fathers want to live up to this perfect father because they've never had the example of one. Since they've never had the example of a father, they create an unrealistic version of a father, which makes it hard to live up to. This flawed perception of a father creates unhealthy pressure and sets the father up for imminent failure. Of course, this is not the reason for all absent fathers, but I believe it is for the majority. A large number of absent fathers did have an example of a father, but it was a poor example. Growing up, you tend to emulate what you see and are around. You become a product of your own environment.

Most absent fathers do not truly realize their actions and the determinant of them because they are duplicating adverse effects that they unconsciously learned growing up. By the time a father realizes that the actions and behaviors that he has adopted over the years were wrong and caused harmful effects, the effects are often irreversible or extremely difficult to reverse. Because of the difficulty this often causes the father to feel the "inadequacy," and they revert back to the familiar position of isolation.

While that is one of the main reasons for absent

fathers, the inability of mothers and fathers to maintain a cordial relationship has to top the list of reasons as well. Again, no excuse but the friction and distance between a separated mother and father can make the father (or mother) discontent about the quality of relationship with their child to the point it pushes them away because the quantity of time is frustrating, therefore minimized. Relationships can indeed be complicated but consider a broken relationship with a child involved. Children are blessings, but we can't overlook the complexity added when a child is born or are a part of a relationship that already has poor communication.

Often there are still emotional feelings and ties between the parents. One of the parents may have hope that the relationship will still work while the other has lost faith in the connection being successful based on the history and current circumstances. This can cause the parent that still desires the relationship to be selfish and adopt an "if I can't have you" attitude and try to keep the child from the other parent or just have resentment towards them. Of course, this is always messy and causes even more damage to the parent's relationship, but ultimately, the child is the one that suffers the greatest. The issue is not always the father's desire to connect and bond with their child, most men desire to be involved, but the disconnection between the parents can cause separation.

One of the most selfish things we can do as parents, and in any relationship, is to only see things from our point of view. Our narrow viewpoint restricts us from seeing what the other person is dealing with and what the driving force is behind their decisions. If we choose to ignore their perspective, then it is impossible to understand.

9

WORTH THE TRIP

Forgiveness has life-changing benefits. Although the thought of forgiveness is daunting, and the actual act and process of forgiving is not fun, it is fruitful. It's liberating and freeing, of course, but there are other benefits. Your forgiveness of others grants you forgiveness.

"For if you forgive men their trespasses, your heavenly Father will also forgive you. However, if you do not forgive men their trespasses, neither will your Father forgive your trespasses" (Matthew 6:14-15 NKJV).

That alone should be enough for us to forgive. I'm sure I'm not the only one that needs forgiveness daily for my sins, known and unknown. We all do! *"If we say that we have not sinned [refusing to admit acts of sin], we make Him [out to be] a liar [by contradicting Him], and His word is not in us" (1 John 1:10 AMP).*

It would be tragic for us to discover that God didn't forgive us of our sins because we held unforgiveness toward someone else. How much more tragic would it be if that unforgiveness we've kept is towards someone who doesn't even own a place in our life anymore or have any effect on our daily living? I don't want anyone or anything standing between me and the fruit of forgiveness of God today, especially if it's in my past and irrelevant to today.

Forgiveness releases authority

Unforgiveness keeps you from producing and harvesting the fullness of your fruit. When you are unable to forgive fully, God is unable to trust you fully. You limit the blessings God has for you because you are unable to use them for His good adequately. God didn't allow me to be a part of a non-profit organization geared towards absent father kids until my heart was no longer tainted by the absence of my father. God withholds what we will ruin; He withholds it until we can see it how He sees it. I viewed the absence of my father as rejection, abandonment, etc. but God considered it an opportunity to have and feel the heart of a child whose father was absent, so I could relate. If I held onto my perception and never took hold to His, I would have never experienced the joy of being a role model or being the light to someone else.

I believe this is evident in several individuals in the Bible, particularly Joseph and David. Imagine if Joseph had not forgiven his brothers, Potiphar's wife, Potiphar, or the butler. Would God have made him the second most powerful man in Egypt behind Pharaoh? I doubt it; Joseph went through his trials so *"that many people would be kept alive [as they are this day]" (Genesis 50:20 AMP)*. If Joseph didn't have the heart to forgive, God might have withheld His authority from Joseph, and he would not have been the second most powerful man in Egypt and been the chosen one to provide for his family during the famine. Joseph's aptitude to forgive placed his family in the best land in Egypt, Goshen, where they were fruitful and multiplied.

David, to me, was one of the most forgiving people that I know of in my life experience! David was a man whose father-in-law, Saul, attempted to kill him on several occasions. David would flee from Saul's attempts on his life but return at Saul's need. I Samuel 18;29, says that Saul became David's enemy continually. After the attempts on David's life by Saul, David would still be Saul's minstrel. Even after Jonathan, David's best friend, told him that Saul was plotting to kill him, David still played music for him. As discussed with David by Jonathan, Saul attempted to kill David again. *"Then Saul sought to pin David to the wall with the spear" (I Samuel 19:10 NKJV).* Can you imagine? How many people do you know that would/can forgive someone for trying to kill them? Numerous times?

Saul was relentless in his pursuit of David and would stop at nothing to take his life. David was not a revengeful man. In Chapter 24 of Samuel, David had the opportunity to get back at Saul and kill him. Even with cheerleaders in his ear, David couldn't kill Saul. He cut a piece of Saul's robe to show Saul that he had the opportunity to end his life but didn't. David even felt bad for doing that, knowing that Saul was anointed by the Lord to be king. When David revealed himself, Saul wept and

"Then he said to David: "You are more righteous than I; for you have rewarded me with good, whereas I have rewarded you with evil. Moreover, you have shown this day how you have dealt well with me; for when the LORD delivered me into your hand, you did not kill me. For if a man finds his enemy, will he let him get away safely? Therefore may the LORD reward you with good for what you have done to me this day. Moreover, now I know indeed that you shall surely be king, and that the kingdom of Israel shall be established in your hand" (1 Samuel 24:17-20 NKJV).

David was already anointed by Samuel to be the next king, but David didn't become king until after his character was proven. David passed the test of revenge. It speaks volumes to your character when you can forgive someone for the offenses they've done against you and can reward them with good when you had the opportunity to do evil.

David was so forgiving of Saul that in 2 Samuel 1:11-12, he mourned over the death of Saul.

"David took hold of his clothes and tore them, and so did all the men who were with him. Moreover, they mourned and wept and fasted until evening for Saul and Jonathan, his son, for the people of the LORD *and the house of Israel because they had fallen by the sword."*

Both David and Joseph experienced hardships and let downs from people. People that were family, people they trusted and highly respected. Throughout the stories of their lives portrayed to us, they had opportunities to allow resentment, bitterness, abandonment, and rejection to be the cause of unforgiveness. Instead, they both chose to forgive, because forgiveness is a decision, and I believe that God gave them authority and led them to be, I think, two of the most influential men in biblical history. David was a young shepherd given the power to be King of Israel that returned the ark to Jerusalem and Joseph was sold into slavery by his brothers but given authority by God to be 2nd in charge of Egypt and a provider for his family during the time of famine.

Forgiveness releases revelation

Forgiveness release revelation. That evening I decided I was going to forgive my father. I immediately began to receive revelation. I began to get downloads from God about His future and hope for me. Even though I wasn't entirely sure of every step or how the visions I had would become a reality, I could see my next. He revealed my next steps through forgiveness. Forgiveness is not easy, so to get to a place of forgiveness and to be able to maintain that forgiveness; we have to look at the promises God has given us about our future. Philippians 3:13 says reach forward to those things which are ahead. When having a hard time forgiving, remember those things that God has revealed to you and why you can't let unforgiveness stand in the way of what's ahead. It is in those moments that I believe God strengthens us to forgive and refreshes His promises by revealing the details of those promises to us.

Unforgiveness blocks communication. If it doesn't entirely block communication, it can cause communication to be one-sided. You have an open line to God, but God is unable to get through to you because your unforgiveness filters what He is saying. If you can't hear what God is saying, then you can't see what He's trying to do. Unforgiveness hinders our ability to listen for the voice of God.

Joseph again provides a great example of forgiveness,

releasing revelation. When Joseph was locked in prison after being accused of trying to sleep with Potiphar's wife, he could have hardened his heart towards everyone and everything, but he didn't. Just because the Lord was with him, showed him mercy and gave him favor doesn't mean he had to accept it and live in it. Have you ever had someone do something against you, and you were upset with them? Then they tried to give you a hug, gift or anything of value but because you were still upset, you didn't want it. Joseph could have responded the same way to God. What has God tried to give you that you missed out on because you weren't in a posture to receive it? Joseph was forgiven of people and his circumstance and was able to get the revelation of the butler and baker's dreams. His revelation of their dreams would eventually get him released from prison.

Lack of revelation keeps you confined to whatever prison you are in. The Greek word for revelation is "apokalupsis," which means uncovering (https://biblehub. com/greek/602.htm). Revelation is the uncovering of the keys needed to open your prison doors. It is your direction, think of it as your GPS. You may know your destination, but do you know how to get there? It's rare for us to get to our destination of life by the route we choose. Many times we encounter speed bumps, stop signs, red lights, detours, potholes, incidents, accidents, bad drivers, slow drivers, reckless drivers, rush hour, roadblocks and roadkill in route to our destiny, but the revelation is your step-by-step guide.

Forgiveness releases freedom

Forgiveness releases freedom. As previously mentioned, Joseph wasn't hindered by offense and unforgiveness. Therefore, he was able to receive a revelation that led to his freedom from prison. Forgiveness breaks you from the bondage and strongholds that oppress and limit you; it removes you from the confinement of your circumstances.

Forgiveness makes you a clean vessel that God can freely move in and through and also helps you to freely navigate in the things of God. *"Where the Spirit of the Lord is, there is liberty" (2 Corinthians 3:17 NKJV).* Where the spirit of the Lord is, there is freedom. When you receive the freedom of God, you hear his voice and can move in the direction He's going and in His timing without restraints. God wants to be able to give to you freely daily; unforgiveness blocks His freedom to give and yours to receive.

Often we mistakenly believe that we are free. For instance, when we get out of a relationship where there was an offense that created unforgiveness, we think that we are free from that experience and unforgiveness because we are in a new, "improved" relationship. The truth of the matter is this; if you haven't forgiven the offenses in the old relationship, then you're not going to be able to forgive the offenses that happen in the new one. You haven't been freed from your prison; you just traded one prison for another.

I believe Bishop Jakes broke this down perfectly in one of his sermons, "Freedom it Cost Too Much" where he preached about the distinction between being free and being free indeed. *"Therefore if the Son makes you free, you shall be free indeed" (John 8:36 NKJV)*. Bishop Jakes spoke about two convicts who escaped from prison. Once they escaped from prison, there was a manhunt for the two men. Even though the men fled from prison, they were still confined and limited to certain things. They couldn't just go into a restaurant or stop at the gas station because they were wanted men. Once they escaped, their mugshots were released to the media and public to identify them as fugitives. If anyone saw them, law enforcement would be notified of their whereabouts, so they could be captured and returned to prison. Even though they weren't physically in prison, they were still prisoners. Their prison just got moved. They were free from that prison, but it was false freedom as Bishop Jakes said they traded one prison for another. This is also true for those you have chosen not to forgive. We lead ourselves to believe that we don't need that person and that could be true, but you do need to forgive, if not you'll trade one prison for another because what you don't master now, will be tested again.

Forgiveness releases favor

Forgiveness releases favor. *Psalm 84:11 says, "The LORD bestows grace and favor and honor; No good thing will He withhold from those who walk uprightly" (AMP)*. Uprightly means to walk in integrity, truth, undefiled, whole, blameless... God presents favor to those who walk free. God favors the forgiver.

Job is probably the best biblical example of this. Job was a man described as being blameless and upright, so much that Satan couldn't touch Job because there was a hedge around him. The Lord blessed the works of Job's hands, and all his possessions increased in the land. Job had it all, a big family and more sheep, camels, oxen, and donkeys than you can count, and he was the greatest of all the people of the East...until God removed his hedge. Job lost everything and even became sick. He had to deal with a wife and friends who told him to curse his God and that he was suffering because he did something wrong and needed to repent. They were wrong and aroused the anger of Job, I'm sure, but certainly God. The only thing that kept them from the wrath of God was a prayer by Job. If Job chose not to forgive them, what would have happened to them? Even more of an important question, what would have happened to Job? Because of Jobs integrity and being upright, he forgave and prayed for his friends. Jobs prayer for his friends released favor because he was restored all that he lost and not only that, but he was restored double what he lost. *"And the* LORD *restored Job's losses when he prayed for his friends. Indeed the* LORD *gave Job twice as much as he had before" (Job 42:10 NKJV).* It's almost impossible to pray a Godly prayer about someone and keep unforgiveness in your heart about them. Your prayers for them will restore what you've lost.

10

UNEXPECTED DELAYS

We all have dealt with betrayal at some point, whether we have been the betrayer or betrayed. Much like offense, betrayal is going to happen during life. Nothing exempts you from betrayal. Some of the most powerful, influential, and wealthiest people have been betrayed.

The greatest man ever to walk the face of the earth was betrayed. Jesus was betrayed by Judas, His treasurer, His CFO, one of the twelve disciples, the men that Jesus chose to teach, impart and walk with Him daily. Jesus not only chose Judas, but He also knew he would betray Him. Judas betrayed Jesus for a small amount of money. Not that you can put a price tag on the Messiah, but it's nothing worse than being betrayed by someone because they can't see the value in you.

Jesus wasn't just betrayed by one of His disciples but two. Peter, probably the most prominent disciple, the disciple that cut off a soldier's ear to defend Jesus also betrayed Him. Peter was one of the disciples that Jesus kept close according to the passage written about the Garden of Gethsemane. Jesus also knew that Peter would betray Him by denying to know Him. *"Jesus said to him, "Assuredly, I say to you that this night before the rooster crows, you will deny Me three times" (Matthew 26:34 NKJV)*. One that was closest to Jesus denied knowing Him during the most critical time of His life to save himself from death, even after he vowed to die with Jesus. "Peter said to Him, "Even if I have to die with You, I will not deny You!" One of the most hurtful things to experience is for someone to make a promise but renege at the time you need their support the most.

If that doesn't exemplify why you're not an exemption from betrayal, maybe this will. Our Father in heaven was betrayed by one of the archangels, Lucifer. Many have labeled Lucifer as the highest angel, but he wasn't satisfied with that. He felt that he possessed power that was equal to God and that he should be God. That lead him to be cast out of heaven, and the angels he was over followed him. Talk about the ultimate betrayal! God trusted Lucifer enough to give him power, authority, and dominion, and Lucifer let pride allow him to believe he was exalted higher than God. Lucifer tried to abuse what he was given to take the position of God.

There are several occurrences of betrayal in the Bible, throughout history, and I'm sure you have witnessed betrayal both directly and indirectly. What interests me about Jesus's betrayers is that He knew they would betray Him. How was He so cool with teaching, traveling, imparting and loving dudes that He knew would betray Him, in some of the shadiest ways? Why did He let it happen? It was all a part of the plan! It had to happen. It's not like Jesus couldn't disappear when they came to seize Him. He's pulled disappearing acts before in groups of people. He surely could have done it again, but it was part of the plan and had to happen. If Judas didn't betray Jesus, then He would have never died on the cross for our sins. It had to happen, just like it has to happen in your life. Certain things in life happen to push you into your next, you can think of it as a chain reaction. If my father was present in my life, I might not know the importance of fatherhood as I do now. Of course, there was confusion and hurt involved, but it opened my eyes to things I would have never seen if my father was present. Whatever betrayal you are facing, please do yourself a favor, accept it, and tell yourself it had to happen. Don't dwell on the who, why, and how you're feeling now. Get ready to move into your next. It had to happen!

11

TEST DRIVE

While writing this book, I was challenged in the area of forgiveness. An offense was done to me that was undeserving, unnecessary, and I did nothing to provoke it. It was an act that would keep most from talking to that person ever again. In the world, I would have been entirely in the right to be unforgiving of this person and never speak to them again, and some would even be in support of me returning the favor. To be truthful, I struggled with this offense. I had several different ill feelings and emotions towards this person, including anger, frustration, disappointment, bitterness, resentment, etc. I had every right to hold on to all of those feelings, and I did. Immediately, I began to feel Proverbs 17:22 in my body. *"A happy heart is good medicine, and a joyful mind causes healing, but a broken spirit dries up the bones."*

Initially, the incident crushed me and affected me emotionally and spiritually. I was distraught wondering why this happened to me, why that person thought it was ok to do, and even why God allowed it to happen. I felt disrespected by a person I had high regard for. I was angry at them and wanted to remain upset about what they did, especially since I couldn't retaliate. Not because I couldn't, but because I knew it wasn't right. So, I remained angry and did the only thing I thought I could do - not speak to them. Unfortunately, in this instance, it wasn't possible since I had to be in proximity of them often...like every day.

After having limited (close to no) communication with them for two or three days but being around them, I began to physically feel the ramifications. My inability to forgive and to forgive them quickly was taking a toll on me. Needless to say, from my viewpoint, that person was carrying on life as usual and appeared careless about my feelings or the effects of their actions. Their nonchalant attitude frustrated and angered me more.

One day I was at home feeling sorry for myself, down and depressed and realized the situation had crippled me for way too long. I believe it's fair to say they were in the wrong but I had to let it go for me. I allowed myself to be bothered by the situation, and it hindered my relationship with God. Not only did I let it separate me from God, but I allowed it to isolate me from people as well. People who could have provided support and godly counsel on how to properly deal with the situation.

12

WHO'S GOING WITH ME?

Unforgiveness leads me to shut down and isolate from God and people. When a person betrays me, I question their loyalty and whether I can continue to trust them or ever trust them again. Those thoughts become contagious and I began to question the loyalty and trust of everyone around me. Ultimately leading me to think I'm better off on my own and consequently down a dangerous path of isolation and depression.

God didn't intend for us to do life alone. There are times that you should be intentional about being alone to rest, reflect, and have quality time with God but not during hardship. We are to seek God first, but we are not to go through it alone. During hardship, we deal with thoughts that sink us in a deeper hole.

When Jesus was at the Garden of Gethsemane with the disciples, he was in a low place. *"...He began to be grieved and greatly distressed. Then He said to them, "My soul is deeply grieved so that I am almost dying of sorrow"* (Matthew 26:37-38 NKJV). To my recollection, this is the first time that we see Jesus weeping for Himself. First time or not, at this point where He is deeply grieved and full of sorrow, close to death, He asks the disciples to do one thing, *"Stay here and watch with me"* (Matthew 26: 38 NKJV). Watch means to be attentive, to keep guard, to keep someone or something under close observation (Merriam Webster). Even Jesus wanted the accountability and community of those He kept close during His weak moment.

Jesus, who already knew the promise and plan of God for Him to die on the cross, asked if death could pass him by. *"O My Father, if it is possible, let this cup pass from Me"* (Matthew 26:39 NKJV). Have you been assigned to do something but once the time came for you actually to do it, an unexpected pressure or overwhelming feeling came over you? This has happened to me. One time I knew that I had to speak in front of people and I was okay with it. I planned out everything I wanted and needed to say, and I was ready. Then the time came for me to speak, and my heart began beating like I just finished running across the country! I wonder if this is how Jesus felt. When Jesus said to the disciples, *"Watch and pray, lest you enter into temptation. The spirit indeed is willing, but the flesh is weak"* (Matthew 26:41

NKJV) was He was also reminding Himself? Indeed His Spirit was willing, that is evident throughout the Bible and in verses 45-46 of this chapter, but did His flesh get weak? Although that doesn't directly have anything to do with forgiveness, it should be acknowledged that Jesus asked his disciples to stay and pray with Him. If you allow forgiveness to isolate you, who is going to help and pray with you? Initially, Jesus asked the disciples (Peter, James, and John) just to watch. Then he returned and asked them to watch and pray. I believe this is significant in regards to accountability during hardship. It stresses the importance of choosing those that can watch (be attentive, guard, observe, listen, see) the difficulty you are going through and be able to precisely pray through it with you. Also, it is crucial to determine who those friends are that you trust with your most intimate moments. All twelve disciples went to Gethsemane, but that is as far as they went. Jesus only took Peter, James, and John further with him.

"Then Jesus came with them to a place called Gethsemane, and said to the disciples, "Sit here while I go and pray over there."Moreover, He took with Him Peter and the two sons of Zebedee" (Matthew 26:36-37 NKJV).

Then verse 39 says, *"He went a little farther."* Although Jesus took Peter, James, and John further with Him, there was still a place that was reserved for only Him and God.

Another revelation I received while studying this scripture was that God ASKED the disciples to watch and pray. He didn't assume they would eventually have the empathy of His need. He didn't wait for them to ask for His needs or what was wrong. The disciples didn't have to dig or pull it out of Jesus. It should be noted that Jesus acknowledged there was an issue to Himself and was vulnerable enough to inform the disciples and then prayed for Himself!

After praying, Jesus checked in with the disciples. That is part of accountability. The disciples didn't check on Jesus; Jesus went to them. The next part is where I think many of us become frustrated with accountability. The disciples were sleeping! Can you believe it? If I was just vulnerable enough to tell you the hardships that I am going through, and your actions show a lack of concern or care, you're no longer my accountability partner. Thanks for your time, but this isn't working for me! I love what Jesus does here though; He gave them advice and instruction for their own lives. *"Watch and pray, lest you enter into temptation" (Matthew 26:41 NKJV).* Then He went back to pray. He went to pray three times, and each time He came back, the disciples were sleeping. I believe Jesus was frustrated and upset with the disciples, but He didn't hold their weakness against them. In verse 46, He says, *"Rise, let US be going."* He knew they were still part of His plan and purpose and didn't let His anger or frustration with them prevent Him from completing it.

13

DESTINATION

I f that happened to me three times consecutively, my response would have been completely different, but Jesus didn't stay in the moment for long, neither did He remain frustrated with the disciples. Why? He had a purpose! Not only did He have a purpose, but His purpose was time sensitive. Before Jesus could even finish His sentence, the next step in His purpose unfolded when Judas came to betray Him. Although none of us want our next step to be the betrayal of a friend, don't let unforgiveness and the lack of accountability keep you from the next step in your purpose. You don't have time. Jesus didn't let His circumstances keep Him from missing the next move of God.

God is more concerned about who is righteous as opposed to who is right. There are times I deserved an apology for offenses done against me but never received them. I found myself waiting for an apology that would never come. I was also opposed to initiating the conversation that may lead to an apology. Most importantly, I was angry and had a hard time getting over the offense. Proverbs 19:11 gave me a different perspective of myself in these situations, and I could no longer continue to leave things as they were.

"A man's discretion makes him slow to anger, and it is his glory to overlook a transgression." Proverbs 19:11 NASB

While writing this book about forgiveness, I asked God why He would have me write a book about something I haven't mastered myself. His response was that forgiveness is not something for you to master. This book is a reminder. Everyone needs to be reminded, and this book will be your life reminder. Forgiveness is not a one-time decision. It's a lifetime choice, you have to make over and over again, and every scenario won't be the same.

There is nothing you can do about the offense. The offense is inevitable, and there is nothing right or wrong you can do to avoid it. As long as you live, there will be someone that says something or someone who does an act or action that insults or attacks you. Especially if you are a believer of Jesus Christ. *"Then He said to the disciples, "It is impossible that no offenses should come, but woe to him through whom they do come" (Luke 17:1 NKJV)!*

What you can control when dealing with the offense is how you respond. Luke 17 continues to say, *"Take heed to yourselves. If your brother sins against you, rebuke him; and if he repents, forgive him" (Luke 17:1-4 NKJV).* This is one of the most difficult parts of offense for me. If someone did something against me, why do I have to go to them? If there is a possibility they are unaware, sure, but what about when they know exactly what they did? Not only does it say I need to go to them but the amplified (AMP) version of the Bible says, *"solemnly warn,"* meaning respectfully. In other words, without an attitude or in an inappropriate manner.

I don't know about anybody else, but that's not how I would choose to handle it. That person needs to know exactly how I feel, and they need to feel what I feel. I love how the word rebukes my process of handling it. Continuing in Luke 17, Jesus questions our faith. *"And the Lord said, if ye had faith as a grain of mustard seed, ye might say unto this sycamine tree, be thou plucked up by the root, and be thou planted in the sea; and it should obey you" (Luke 17:6 KJV).* In this passage, Jesus is saying that if you believe, even with the slightest belief, you can forgive. In the scripture, He references the sycamine tree. The sycamine tree has one of the deepest root structures, making it difficult to uproot. Jesus says that if you have the slightest faith, the things that are deeply rooted and hard to remove will be removed.

Could your unforgiveness be because you lack faith that you can forgive?

Since offense is inevitable and we have faith to remove it, why does it remain in us? It's because we mismanage it. If you don't handle offense quickly and adequately, it is used to manipulate the truth and create strife within yourself and others. With mismanagement, the enemy will make something out of nothing. The enemy is a master at making a mountain out of a molehill. Don't let offense elevate into bitterness, unforgiveness and even hatred. You can't do anything about being wronged. It is in the past, and you can't change it, you can only respond well.

14

DETOURS

There are ways to handle unforgiveness and offense properly. If the offense is not handled correctly, it will be used to:

Destroy purposeful, covenant relationships

I'm not offended by everybody. Two different people could do the same thing to me, and I can be hurt by one and not the other. For example, if a stranger insulted me, I would be unbothered, but if my mother insulted me, then I would surely be offended. The people you are most offended by are people that you are in close relationship with. The people that hurt you the most are the people that are closest to you. Most of the time, you are close to them because there is value in the relationship, and the relationship is important to you and your purpose. These relation-ships are prime candidates for the enemy to destroy. *"The thief does not come except to steal, and to kill, and to destroy" (John 10:10 NKJV).* The enemy desires to keep you from your purpose, and God has attached our purpose to others. If God has to partner with us to carry out His purpose on earth, then surely we have to partner with one another. The enemy understands this better than we do and will always attack our relationships that serve God's purpose.

"Again, I say to you that if two of you agree on earth concerning anything that they ask, it will be done for them by My Father in heaven. For where two or three are gathered together in My name, I am there in the midst of them" (Matthew 18:19-20 NKJV).

This is an area where your discernment must kick in because every separation is not from the enemy or an attack by the enemy. There is an end to every time and season. Our job is to understand whether it is the will of God or an attempt by the enemy to create distraction, discord, and division.

Distracts you from your purpose/destiny

The offense is a tool of distraction. There is no doubt that offense and distractions are going to happen, so why are we so easily sidetracked when it occurs? Offense's objective is to divert your focus. Hurt is the first result of offense but your hurt branches out to questions and thoughts that you may never understand. When we occupy ourselves with pain and all that's attached to it, it keeps us from purpose and places us in a cycle. It causes us to have a difficult time directing our thoughts toward the steps needed to reach our purpose. Our minds are subject to draw conclusions and answers to questions that will never be resolved, using valuable time and energy.

Purpose isn't a one-time move or one step. It is a process that involves multiple steps and your undivided attention. In every step of the process, offensiveness can attempt to creep in and prevent or delay you from reaching your purpose and the fullness of it. It is your job to be intentional and not distracted from your purpose.

King David was offended by the Lord in 2nd Samuel 6. He gathered all the choice men of Israel to bring the ark of God to Jerusalem. During the journey, *"Uzzah reached out [with his hand] to the ark of God and took hold of it because the oxen [stumbled and] nearly overturned it. Moreover, the anger of the LORD burned against Uzzah, and God struck him there for his irreverence, and he died there by the ark of God. David became angry and grieved and offended because of the LORD's outburst against Uzzah, and that place has been called Perez-Uzzah (outburst against Uzzah) to this day"* (2 Samuel 6:6-8 AMP).

God hurt David, the one he was moving the ark for. Like most of us, David began to question himself because he was hurt. "How can the ark of the Lord come to me?" David asked. I'm sure he internally asked more questions in his mind as we all do. "What did I do wrong?" "Am I even supposed to be doing this?" "Am I even good enough to do this?" Like David, we allow our anger, grief, and offense to distract us from our purpose. David's purpose at that moment was to bring the ark back to Jerusalem, but like most of us, David got distracted by the hurdles and obstacles we face in route to our destination, in David's case it was offense resulting from the death of Uzzah.

David lost focus on his purpose and completely abandoned it, as written in verse 9. What have you completely abandoned because you were offended? What were you so focused on that was the will of God, but you allowed the distraction of offense, whether from the enemy or God, to cause you to completely abandon it and even forget about it?

David was unwilling to move the ark and left it at Obed-edom's house. He left his purpose with someone else. Who have you left your purpose with? David forgot about the ark until he got word that Obed-Edom and all his household were blessed because of it. Of course, we want others to be blessed but not at the expense of our disobedience. God owns everything, so surely there is enough for all of us. People don't need to be blessed because I forfeited my purpose. Although God can use anyone to complete His purpose, He has chosen you, and no one can do your purpose like you. You were created for it! Don't let your offense make you negligent to your purpose.

Creates competition and impure motives

When you are offended by someone, and it is mishandled, the motives of your purpose can change. It is crucial to make sure your motives are for God and not to prove others wrong, prove to them that you could do it without them or for the validation of others. You are not called to your purpose to prove someone wrong. If your motivation is to impress or to have your good deeds seen by the person or small group that offended you, you are not only distracted, but your motives are impure, and you are not ready to walk in the fullness of your purpose.

For instance, writing this book was God's purpose. If I wrote this book to assassinate my father's character, then my motives would be wrong and impure. My motives for this book are to bring light to fatherlessness and to encourage those who are and were fatherless to forgive their fathers by sharing my testimony and the process I went through to forgive my father. God's purpose wouldn't change in either instance, but my motives could. Your purpose should never be to hurt someone or boast yourself but to help others. What good was your pain if you don't use it to help others?

Your purpose requires your humility, and you can't be humble and offended. You must be submissive to serve those directly affected by your purpose, and sometimes those people are the ones who have offended you and those that will hurt you. Your humility will allow you to grant them grace, so you don't become distracted and lose sight of your purpose and those you are called to. Your purpose will involve you considering the interests and needs of others.

"Do nothing from selfish ambition or conceit, but in humility, count others more significant than yourselves. Let each of you look not only to his interests but also to the interests of others" (Philippians 2:3-4 ESV).

Be careful of your why. Why you set that goal or why you want to accomplish that task. It's possible for offense and unforgiveness to fuel your accomplishments, and you become a product of pride. When your accomplishments are rooted in the pride of impressing or outdoing people and not the purpose of God, you are bound for destruction. *"Before destruction, the heart of a man is haughty, and before honor is humility" (Proverbs 18:21 NKJV).* Humility comes before honor. To be honored God's way, forgive your offenders, so your motives are pure.

We can look at the story of Cain and Abel and see how Cain let offense distract him, rule over him and create a deadly rival with his brother. Cain chose to be offended and not humble. Cain had the same rights to the respect of the Lord as Abel because God is not a respecter of persons.

"In truth, I perceive that God shows no partiality. However, in every nation whoever fears Him and works righteousness is accepted by Him" (Acts 10:34-35 NKJV).

Cain only needed to do well, according to Genesis 4:7. Even though he didn't offer his first fruit initially, the passage implies that he would have other chances to do so. I love that God gives us second chances; third, fourth, God gives us unlimited chances by grace. Cain, unfortunately, chose to allow the offense to distract him from offering his first fruit the next time, to killing what was connected to him, his brother. Don't let offense kill what you're supposed to be connected to. Don't sever your connections because you allowed it to create competition.

Discord

When you let your guard down to unforgiveness and offense, it allows the opportunity for discord to take place. Discord prevents the parties involved from coming to an agreement or conclusion. Agreeing in every matter is not always the result of every problem, but discord will keep you from agreeing to disagree. When you're able to agree to disagree, you can move on from the situation, leaving unforgiveness, offense or any other ill feelings behind.

Eliminating discord from the matter also permits God to be a part of the relationship, partnership, and plans. Matthew 18 talks about this and how God is in the midst of those that agree in His name. Discord keeps us from agreeing, and when we are unable to agree, it hinders God's manifestation and presence in our plans. We need God's presence in our plans. Just because we have plans or things that are going good in our life, doesn't mean they are reaching full potential. The agreement permits the full manifestation of God to take place and His plans for us to achieve fullness.

Deception

How does deception play into mishandling unforgiveness and offense? Deceit is usually an offense committed by the offender, but the offended can be deceived as well. The offender, in many cases, causes offense and unforgiveness in some way. The offended can misguide themselves by believing that since they were offended, the onus is entirely on the offender. This could be no further from the truth, and the offended has deceived themselves.

"Moreover, if your brother sins against you, go and tell him

his fault between you and him alone" (*Matthew 18:15a NKJV*). Matthew 18:15 shows us that the offended is the first to act in the reconciliation of the offense. Why? *"If they listen to you, you have won them over"* (*Matthew 18:15b NKJV*). Winning your brother over means that you have gained their respect. You gained their respect because you brought the truth to light. Holding an offense to yourself is deceitful to the offender, especially in cases, where they may not be aware that they have committed an offense against you. Pointing out the offense keeps you both from being deceived. The offender is not deceived believing things are kosher, and the offended doesn't have false beliefs or assumptions about what the offender did.

That deceit keeps you in the spirit of the offense. When you don't truly shed light on it, you deceive yourself into thinking its ok, it's not that serious, or you'll hold resentment towards that person because you haven't dealt with the truth and confronted the deceit.

15

DO IT FOR YOU

Dealing with the offense and the offender can be a hard task, especially in cases where the offenses are habitual. How do you deal with someone who knows they have offended you and they continue to offend you carelessly? In cases like this, it is important to ultimately remember that an intentional offense against you is also against God. It is not for us to get back at our offenders but rather to do good to them. *"Repay no one evil for evil. Have regard for good things in the sight of all men" (Romans 12-17 NKJV)*. I know, much easier said than done. It is much easier for God to handle our offenders than for us too. Leaving vengeance to God should bring comfort to you, knowing that you don't have to handle it, but He will. *"Beloved, do not avenge yourselves, but rather give place to wrath; for it is written, "Vengeance is Mine, I will repay," says the Lord" (Romans 12:19 NKJV).*

I can't bypass how hard this is to do. Naturally, we feel we need to defend and stick up for ourselves. Most of us have been taught this all of our life. I know many of us can remember our parents saying to us during our elementary and middle school years, "if somebody hits you, hit them back." Some of us have been taught to fight back, and all of our lives we have been fighting back. Some of the things we fight about are so irreverent but standing up for ourselves has become such an instinct that we don't consider the value of the fight.

Romans 12 challenges the reason for our fights and how to fight. It states that we shouldn't do evil to those that have done evil to us but rather do good to them. It also shows us how doing good to them will overcome the evil that has been done. *"Therefore if your enemy is hungry, feed him; If he is thirsty, give him a drink; For in so doing, you will heap coals of fire on his head. Do not be overcome by evil but overcome evil with good" (Romans 12:20-21 NKJV).*

When we choose to fight our battles with good, we overcome the offense that was done. Not only do we over-come evil, but the offender will be affected by our good-ness. "You will heap coals of fire on his head," some versions translate this to feeling the shame of what they've done. Your good can be effective in changing that person for good opposed to repaying their evil, which would make them worse.

Their offense against you is also against God, but your response could also be against God. If you repay evil with evil, you have opposed the word and way of God. You can't allow the offense of a person to cause you to be in opposition to God. Deuteronomy 28 lists the blessings and curses of obeying and disobeying the word of God. Repaying good for evil is obeying the word of God and gives you the blessings of God. Don't let your response to evil disqualify you from the blessings of God.

16

THE JOURNEY TO PERFECTING FORGIVENESS

F orgiveness is not easy but essential for your life and the life of others. For so many years, I let unforgiveness obstruct me from the fullness of life that was not only available to me but was meant for me to have. I let the actions of someone else keep me from enjoying life and getting the most out of it.

I can't say it enough; forgiveness is not for the other person it's for you. You deserve to have joy, peace, love, and the blessings of God. You've allowed unforgiveness to steal enough from you; it's occupied enough of your time and thoughts. It's time for you to get your life back and take it by force.

Of course, forgiveness is not easy, but it can become facile, like anything else, through practice. Forgive people for small and minor offenses throughout your day. Practice going to them and explaining your offense, I know it gets awkward and may even seem pointless sometimes, but it builds you to be able to deal with significant offenses when they occur. Forgiveness also becomes a lifestyle.

Forgiveness isn't a one-time occurrence but should be something that you do all the time. We should live lives of forgiveness. It would be hard for me to run a mile if I haven't run in a year, but if I've been running consistently, the mile will be more comfortable to run. Eventually, a mile would be easy, and I could stretch myself to do two miles. The same principle applies to forgiveness, be consistent. The more you do it; it increases your capacity to do more.

Nothing happens overnight. Forgiveness is a lifelong process. As long as we live, there will be an opportunity for offense and betrayal to happen, especially if we continue to grow and become accessible to more people and different walks of life. Over and over again, we'll find ourselves going through the process of forgiveness. I believe the offenses will get easier to handle, but I can't promise that, but I do believe you'll be able to handle it better each time. Each offense is different and requires a different level of forgiveness, but I believe your last time of forgiveness has prepared you for the next one. It's a journey to perfecting forgiveness. You will never perfect it, but each time you'll be better. Give yourself the grace to perfect it each time at your level of experience.

In perfecting forgiveness, first, learn to forgive yourself. Don't blame yourself for things you couldn't control. You couldn't have done anything differently. Nothing you said or did could have prevented the offense. Remember it had to happen. The best thing you can do for yourself is to forgive you. Don't blame yourself because you made a bad choice, said the wrong thing, did the wrong thing and didn't surround yourself with the right people, or whatever your reason is. This is your first life; you're allowed to make mistakes. You're learning like everyone else. Forgive yourself!

I pray that this book has been a blessing to someone and has helped you deal with unforgiveness. May you be free from the bondage and strongholds of unforgiveness and live a prosperous life full of love, joy, peace, and freedom!

APPENDIX A

There is a song by Tina Campbell named "Too Hard Not to." I love this song and think it sums up forgiveness in a beautiful way. Here's an excerpt from the song:

Maybe you feel entitled
'Cause this should have never, ever happened to you
And maybe you've tried to let it go
But letting go just ain't never easy to do
And maybe you feel you'll end up with another broken heart
Trying to face something that seems way too hard
But it's too hard to hold on to all of the pain
And it's too hard to relive it over and over again
It's too hard when the memories have control over you
Some say it's too hard to forgive
I say it's too hard not to

It's too hard not to
It's too hard not to

I believe this verse and chorus describe the feelings of many dealing with unforgiveness. Most feel entitled to be unforgiving towards offenders because they feel the offense shouldn't have happened to them. They feel undeserving o be offended. Many people know they need to let it go, but as the lyrics say "letting go just ain't never easy to do," especially when there is a chance it may happen again. You build up a wall to the offender in that circumstance, and you build up a wall to keep you protected in future circumstances. Dealing with that offense and forgiving is hard, but what we don't realize is it's even harder holding onto the pain of the situation and reliving it over and over again. That situation and the memories of it control you and how you handle future circumstances. It's hard to forgive, I agree with that, but it's harder not too [forgive]. Living in the pain of memories and unforgiveness is too hard.

APPENDIX B

Prayer of Forgiveness: Who do you need to forgive?

I, _____ , forgive (insert your name here) myself and _____ (insert person(s) name here) for _____. (insert the offense or what they did to you here)

    I release myself from the person(s) involved in this offense and the power I have given this offense. I now render it powerless in my life. I will no longer allow these people or this offense to have control or authority over me and my life. I cut all ties from this offense, and I am now free from it and free the individuals that were involved. I forgive them. Me forgiving them does not condone or acknowledge their behaviors as right or acceptable but releases them from their wrongdoing just as I have been. I will bring every thought of this offense into captivity. I will speak the word of God over myself. I am not my past, I am not my past mistakes, I am not my past failures, and I am not what people have done to me. I am free and whom the Son sets free, is free indeed.

God, thank you for coming into my heart and making the hard places of my heart flesh again. Thank You for giving me a forgiving heart and thank You for teaching me how to properly deal with the offense and Your people.

APPENDIX C

DECLARATIONS

Now that you have forgiven those who offended or hurt you. Speak declarations over yourself. Here are a few but come up with some specific to you and the call on your life!

I am a changed man/woman! (2 Corinthians 5:17)

I am loved by God! (John 3:16)

I can do all things and will not fail! (Philippians 4:13)

I was fearfully and wonderfully made! (Psalm 139:14)

I have a future! (Jeremiah 29:11)

I have been chosen! (1 Peter 2:9)

I will see the goodness of the Lord! (Psalm 27:13)

God cares about me! (Psalm 8:4)

God is with you! (Deuteronomy 31:6)

I am an overcomer! (Romans 8:37)

I have a purpose! (Ephesians 2:10)

Someone needs me and is depending on me! (Genesis 50:20)

I was made for this! (Psalm 139:16)

REFERENCES

America's Families and Living Arrangements: 2012. Population Characteristics. https://www.census.gov/prod/2013pubs/p20-570.pdf. Accessed 17 May 2019.

"Apokalupsis.," https://biblehub.com/greek/602.htm

Campbell, Tina. "Too Hard Not To." Lyrics. It's Still Personal. Campbell Kids Publishing, EMI April Music Inc, It's Tea Tyme, WB Music Corp., 2017.

Galatians 5:17 AMP - "Walk By The Spirit - It Was For This ..." *BibleGateway*. N.p., n.d. Web. 27 Jun. 2019 https://www.biblegateway.com/passage/?search=Galatians%205&version=AMP.

HuffPost. Absent Fathers: An Absentee Dad Explains Why Men Leave Their Children. 5 May 2013. (https://www. huffingtonpost.com/2013/05/08/absent-fathers-dad-why-men-leave-children_n_3231932.html). Accessed 3 August 2018.

John 10:27 NKJV "My Sheep Listen To My Voice; I Know Them, And ..." *BibleGateway*. N.p., n.d. Web. 27 Jun. 2019 https://www.biblegateway.com/passage/?search=John+10%3A27&version=NKJV

Luke 17:1 - NKJV - "Then He Said To The Disciples, "it Is ..." *BibleGateway*. N.p., n.d. Web. 27 Jun. 2019 https://www.biblegateway.com/passage/?search=Luke+17%3A1&version=NKJV

Luke 17:1-10 - NKJV - "Then He Said To The Disciples, "it ..." *BibleGateway*. N.p., n.d. Web. 27 Jun. 2019 https://www.biblegateway.com/passage/?search=Luke+17%3A1-10&version=NKJV

Madamenoire. Are You Coddling Your Son Or Raising Him To Be A Son? 1 August 2011. http://madamenoire.com/62746/are-you-coddling-your-son-or-raising-him-to-be-a-man/2/. Accessed 3 August 2018.

Matthew 12:45 AMP, "Then He Goes and Takes With Him..." *BibleGateway*. N.p., n.d. Web. 27 Jun. https://www. biblegateway.com/passage/?search=MATTHEW+12% 3A45&version=NKJV

Matthew 18:19-20 NKJV - "Again, I Tell You Truly That If Two Of You ..." *BibleGateway*. N.p., n.d. Web. 27 Jun. 2019 https://www.biblegateway.com/passage/?search= MATTHEW+26%3A37&version=NKJV

Matthew 26:37-38 NKJV - "And He Took With Him Peter And The Two ..." Insert Name of Site in Italics. N.p., n.d. Web. 12 Jun. 2019 https://www.biblegateway.com/passage/? search=MATTHEW+26%3A37&version=NKJV

Matthew 26:39 NKJV - "Going A Little Farther, He Fell Facedown And ..." *BibleGateway*. N.p., n.d.Web. 27 Jun. Web. 12 Jun. 2019, https://www.biblegateway.com/passage/? search=Matthew+26%3A39&version=NKJV

National Center for Fathering: Engaging Fathers. Enriching Lives. 2018. http://www.fathers.com/statistics- and-research/the-extent-of-fatherlessness/. Accessed 3 August 2018.

Philippians 2:3-4 ESV - "Do Nothing From Selfish Ambition Or ..." *BibleGateway*. N.p., n.d. Web. 27 Jun. 2019 https://www.

biblegateway.com/passage/?search=Philippians+2%3A3-4&version=ESV

Philippians 3:12-14 NKJV – "Not that I have already attained…" *BibleGateway* N.p., n.d. Web. 12 Jun. 2019, https://www.biblegateway.com/verse/en/Philippians%203%3A12.

Proverbs 3:7 AMP "Do Not Be Wise In Your Own Eyes; Fear The …" *BibleGateway*. N.p., n.d. Web. 27 Jun. 2019 https://www.biblegateway.com/passage/?search=Proverbs+3%3A7&version=AMP

Proverbs 3:7-8 AMP - "It Will Be Health To Your Body [your …" *BibleGateway*. N.p., n.d. Web. 27 Jun. 2019 https://www.biblegateway.com/passage/?search=Proverbs+3%3A7-8&version=AMP

Proverbs 14:30 AMP - "A Calm And Peaceful And Tranquil …" *BibleGateway*. N.p., n.d. Web. 27 Jun. 2019 https://www.biblegateway.com/passage/?search=Proverbs+14%3A30&version=AMP.

Proverbs 18:12 NKJV - "Before Destruction The Heart of a Man Is Haughty …" *BibleGateway*. N.p., n.d. Web. 27 Jun. 2019 https://www.biblegateway.com/passage/?search=Proverbs+18%3A12&version=NKJV

Romans 12:20-21 NKJV "For In So Doing, You Will Heap Burning ..." *BibleGateway*. N.p., n.d. Web. 27 Jun. 2019 https:// www.biblegateway.com/passage/?search=Romans+12% 3A20&version=NKJV

Psalm 27:13 "Still I Am Certain To See The Goodness Of The ..." *BibleGateway*. N.p., n.d. Web. 27 Jun. 2019 https:// www.biblegateway.com/passage/?search=psalm+27%3A13& version=NKJV

Psalm 139:13-16 - NKJV - "For You Formed My Inward Parts ..." *BibleGateway*". N.p., n.d. Web. 12 Jun. 2019 https://www. biblegateway.com/passage/?search=Psalm+139%3A13-16& version=NKJV

Romans 8:1 NKJV "Therefore, There Is Now No Condemnation For ..." *BibleGateway*. N.p., n.d. Web. 27 Jun. 2019 https://www.biblegateway.com/passage/?search= ROMANS+8%3A1&version=NKJV

Romans 12 NKJV - "Living Sacrifices To God - I Beseech ..." *BibleGateway*. N.p., n.d. Web. 27 Jun. 2019 https://www. biblegateway.com/passage/?search=romans+12& version=NKJV

Romans 12:2 NLT - "Don't Copy The Behavior And Customs ..." *BibleGateway*. N.p., n.d. Web. 27 Jun. 2019 https://www.

biblegateway.com/passage/?search=ROMANS+ 12%3A2&version=NLT

2 Timothy 1:7 NKJV "for God Hath Not Given Us The Spirit Of ..." *BibleGateway* . N.p., n.d. Web. 12 Jun. 2019 https:// www.biblegateway.com/passage/?search=2+timothy+1% 3A7&version=NKJV

Made in the USA
Las Vegas, NV
08 January 2022